I'LL TAKE
THE HIGH
ROAD

JOHN PHILLIPS

Developed as a study course by Emmaus Correspondence School, founded in 1942.

Published by:

Emmaus Correspondence School
(A division of ECS Ministries)
PO Box 1028
Dubuque, IA 52004-1028
www.ecsministries.org

Revised 2005

ISBN 0-940293-23-4

© 1985, 2005 ECS Ministries

Cover by Ragont Design, Barrington, IL

Printed in the United States of America

Instructions to Students

A little girl was once lost in the great city of London. A helpful policeman tried to find out where she lived but the little girl did not even know her address. So he began to name and describe the great landmarks of London in the hope something would register with the child. The Houses of Parliament and Westminster Abbey, Buckingham Palace and St. Paul's, Tower Bridge and Trafalgar Square—place after place he described. But the little girl was not moved by any of these. Presently the policeman mentioned Charing Cross and the great stone cross on the road. At once the little girl dried her tears. She looked up at the policeman and said, "Sir, if you take me to the cross I can find my way home from there!"

The road to heaven begins at the cross, the place where Jesus died to bring us to God. If we come to the cross and put our trust in Christ we can find our way home from there! We begin life anew.

This course is intended to help you measure your progress along the Christian pathway. We trust you will study from chapter to chapter and grow confident that you are indeed taking the High Road.

Lessons You Will Study

Course Components

This course has two parts: this study course and a separate exam booklet.

How to Study

This study has twelve chapters that will greatly help you. Each chapter has its own exam. Begin by asking God to open your heart to receive the truths He would teach you from His Word. Read the chapter through at least twice, once to get a general idea of its contents and then again, slowly, looking up all the Scripture references.

Begin studying immediately, or if you are in a group, as soon as the group begins. We suggest that you keep a regular schedule by trying to completing one chapter per week.

Exams

In the exam booklet there is one exam for each chapter (Exam 1 covers chapter 1 of the course). Do not answer the questions by what you think or have always believed. The questions are designed to find out if you understand the material and the Scripture verses given in the course.

After you have completed each chapter, review the related exam, and see how well you know the answers. If you find that you are having difficulty answering the questions, review the material until you think you can answer the questions.

How Your Exams are Graded

Your instructor will mark any incorrectly answered questions. You will be referred back to the place in the Bible or textbook where the correct answer is to be found. After finishing this course with a passing average, you will be awarded a certificate.

If you enrolled in a class, submit your exam papers to the leader or secretary of the class who will send them for the entire group to the Correspondence School.

See the back of the Exam Booklet for more information on returning the exams for grading.

1

BEING BORN TWICE

There lives in Rome, Italy an elderly Indian man (he was a Hindu) and his wife, a native born Italian.

At one time he owned a chain of Jewelry stores in the Hilton and other top-flight hotels in Egypt. He prospered so much that he decided to sell his stores in Egypt, and move to Italy. Once in Italy he opened a store in one of Rome's fashionable hotels. He was getting on in years so he invited his son to join him in Rome. He eventually turned over the store and much of his wealth to his son to manage. Before long he discovered that his son was embezzling funds, using his power of attorney to systematically rob his aged parents. It was only by chance that the father was able to salvage anything for his own personal needs. The behavior of his son caused great sorrow, disappointment and anger.

Then, one day, while watching television, the couple happened to pick up a Bible Broadcast in Italian. They became interested and wrote for a schedule of broadcasts in any or all of the half dozen languages they spoke. Soon afterwards the old gentleman discovered he could obtain an Emmaus Bible Course. He wrote for it, and began to seriously study the Bible. He became increasingly aware of his own need to personally meet the Master and wrote for someone to come and visit him. The man who distributes these courses in Italy went to see this aged Hindu and introduced him to the Lord Jesus.

Soon afterwards the wife also found peace with God through the Lord Jesus Christ. They were born once again, this time into the family of God. The transforming miracle took place. The two of them then systematically studied God's Word together seeking to grow in grace and increase in the knowledge of God. Now this aged couple have new treasures to replace their lost material wealth. They have Bibles in three or four languages, Bible study courses, new life in Christ. And, of course, they are praying for the son who did them such wrong.

Does it work? Does it last? This aged couple are living proof that it does. The life changing Son of the living God became the center and sum of their lives. Their experience demonstrates one basic fact about the Christian life; it is a supernatural life imparted and maintained by a miracle of God. The very life of God is transmitted to the believer in Jesus Christ (Titus 3:5). He receives a new nature, a new heart, and a new life.

The Christian life is a supernatural life. It begins with a supernatural experience known as the new birth. It is continued with the supernatural aid of the Holy Spirit of God. It is terminated supernaturally at death by entrance into the life beyond. It is assumed that you who study this course have already experienced the new birth. If not we suggest you write to the source from which you obtained this course for an introductory course such as *Men Who Met the Master* (six chapters). But because this introduction into the Christian life is so essential and so miraculous and because everything else in the Christian life hinges on it, we are going to spend one lesson reviewing what happens when a person has this supernatural encounter with God, which results in regeneration (the new birth).

The Requirement

1. The Requirement Expressed

Jesus was most emphatic about the need for the new birth. He was speaking once to a devout, conscientious, Bible-believing, religious and orthodox Jew named Nicodemus. To this man who, one would have thought, had all the requirements to assure him a place in the kingdom of God, Jesus said: "You must be born again. . . . Except a man be born again he cannot see the kingdom of God."

The Lord Jesus did not say to Nicodemus, "You *should* be born again." Nor did He say, "Would you *like* to be born again?" He said, "You *must* be born again." It is one of the great imperatives of the Christian faith. This, no doubt, is why the great preacher of a past generation, George Whitfield, when asked by a woman why he always preached "You must be born again," replied, "Madam, because you MUST be born again!"

2. The Requirement Explained

It is not hard to see why this requirement is mandatory. For the sake of illustration imagine the following situation. A lumberjack once lived deep in the royal forest. He carried about with him in his heart a deep desire to see the king and to ask of him a special favor. One day, his great opportunity came, for the king passed right by where the woodcutter was at work. He flung himself at the feet of the king and said, "Your majesty, I am one of your most loyal subjects. I am a law-abiding, honest, moral, clean-living, upright and religious man. I am a good husband to my wife, a good father to my children and a good neighbor and friend. I have never done anyone any harm. I always pay my debts. I am charitable towards the poor and the needy. Therefore, your majesty, I expect that you will now take me back with you to your palace, place me in your family and treat me as one of your own sons!"

You would conclude that the man was a fool. Obviously, to have a right to live in the palace as one of the king's sons he would need to be born into the king's family. Yet there are many people who assume a similar attitude towards God. In effect, if not in so many words, they say to God, "Oh God, I do the best I can. I believe the Bible and pray, give to the poor and attend church. I try to live a decent, moral, respectable life. I try to live by the golden rule of loving my neighbor. Therefore I expect that, when I die, you will take me to heaven and treat me as one of your own sons." To all such pleas God has only one word: "You must be born again." To have a place in God's home and right of access to heaven you have to be born into the family of God.

The Reason

A great preacher R. A. Torrey was once talking to a man who thought his own good works were sufficient to get him to heaven. He argued that he lived a much better life than many Christians he knew. Dr. Torrey drew two rectangles in the sawdust on the floor of the tent in which they were standing. "This first rectangle," he said, "represents the state of the man who has been born twice. We will call it *'The State of Regeneracy.'* The second one we will call *'The State of Unregeneracy.'*

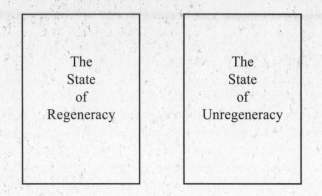

The State of Regeneracy	The State of Unregeneracy

"Now," he continued, "imagine for a moment that you are in the United States, say in the State of Colorado. You might be on Pike's Peak 14,110 feet above sea level, you might be living at sea level, you might be in a mine hundreds of feet below sea level, or you might be anywhere in between. But you are still in the State of Colorado.

"Just so with these two 'States' I have depicted in the sawdust. A man, in the State of Unregeneracy, might be living high up on the mountains of morality, he might be living an average, fairly decent life, he might be living low down in open sin or he might be living anywhere in between. But he is still in the State of Unregeneracy. He was born into that 'State' and there he remains until he is born again.

"On the other hand, a born-again (regenerate) person lives in the State of Regeneracy. He might be living a victorious, fruitful, dynamic and effective Christian life, he might be living an average Christian life from not drawing from God's resources, he might be living a defeated Christian life or he might be living anywhere in between. But he is still in the State of Regeneracy. For you to say that you are living a moral life better than some Christians you know is beside the point. In which 'State' are you living? Have you been born again? Are you in the State of Regeneracy?"

The reason we need to be born again is because we were born all wrong the first time. When God decided to create a race of men He said: "Let us make man in our image, after our likeness" (Genesis 1:26).[1] This He did. He created a perfect pair and placed them in a perfect environment. But then our first parents sinned. (We often call this "the Fall.") When the

---

[1] References such as this one refer to Bible quotations. If you are not familiar with them, use the index page of your Bible. Numbers refer first to the chapter, then to the verse.

Bible later speaks about Adam's descendants it says, "And Adam . . . begat a son in his own likeness, after his image . . ." (Genesis 5:3). Adam's descendants were born, not in the image and likeness of God but in the image and likeness of fallen Adam. To borrow the expressive language of the Psalmist, we were "shapen in iniquity" (Psalm 51:5).

We are sinners by birth, by choice and by practice. The Bible says, "Your iniquities have separated between you and your God and your sins have hid His face from you, that He will not hear" (Isaiah 59:2). God's estimate of the unregenerate heart of man is devastating indeed. He says, "The heart is deceitful above all things, and desperately wicked: who can know it? I the Lord" (Jeremiah 17:9, 10). Sin has wrecked and ruined this world and God will not permit it in heaven. That is why the new birth is essential. Somehow the question of our sin has to be dealt with in a way satisfactory to God. He has to perform a miracle which will transfer us from Adam's family, into which we were born by nature, and place us in His family with a new nature pleasing to him.

Some years ago a medical doctor was dying. He had been an eminent man in his profession but he was not ready to die. A Christian friend was by his bedside trying to explain to him God's way of salvation. He soon made mention of the new birth. At once the doctor pulled himself up on his pillow. "Why, that's exactly what I need," he said. "I need to be born again. I've seen many a baby born and one thing is sure—a baby has no past; it only has a future. How can I be born again?"

The Rule

"How can a man be born when he is old?" asked Nicodemus (John 3:4). The Lord Jesus explained to him that physical laws produced physical birth and spiritual laws produced spiritual birth. He said, "That which is born of the flesh is flesh; and that which is born of the Spirit is spirit" (John 3:6).[2] The actual rule or principle which brings about spiritual birth, birth into God's family, is stated in these words: "He (the Lord Jesus Christ) came unto his own (the Jews) and his own received him not. But as many as received him, to them (whether Jew or Gentile) gave he the power to become the sons of God, even to them that believe on his name; which were born, not of blood, nor of the will of the flesh, nor of the will of man, but of God" (John 1:11-13). Let us examine these verses in detail.

1. Three Startling Contradictions

There are three things which being regenerated is *not*. The three negatives of verse thirteen cut away all false hopes. It is:

➤ **Not by Family Influences**

➤ **Not by Fine Intentions**

➤ **Not by Fleshly Impulses**

a. First, being born again has nothing to do with *family influence*. It is "not of blood." It is not of human descent. Just because my father was a Christian does not make me one. God has many children but He has no grandchildren. Being born into God's family is a matter of personal, individual experience. It is not something inherited from Christian parents. The only thing we inherit from our parents is a sinful nature. Nobody has to teach his children to be rebellious, disobedient, self-willed, quarrelsome or dishonest. Such traits are inherited by natural birth.

The Lord Jesus told of a certain rich man who died and went to a place of separation from God. There, in his torment, he could see Abraham afar off. He prayed to him, pleading a relationship to Abraham and hoping that family influence might help him. "Father Abraham!" he cried. The family connections were there all right but they did not help the lost man. "Son, remember" was Abraham's ultimate reply, throwing the man back upon the

---

[2] Jesus used a much misunderstood phrase when speaking to Nicodemus about the new birth. He said, "Except a man be born of water and of the Spirit, he cannot enter into the kingdom of God" (John 3:5). Many interpretations have been suggested:

a. Some think it is an allusion to the water of cleansing of Ezekiel 36:25.

b. Others see in the reference an allusion to physical birth as an illustration of spiritual birth since delivery of a babe is actually effected "out of" water.

c. Many are convinced it is a reference to Christian baptism. But this ordinance had not yet been instituted by the Lord so reference to it in such a casual way would have meant nothing to Nicodemus. In any case the new birth is not dependent on Christian baptism which is, as Peter puts it, "the answer of a good conscience toward God" (1 Peter 3:21).

d. Another likely interpretation is that the Lord was alluding to the work of John the Baptist. Nicodemus was thoroughly familiar with John's preaching and with the fact that he baptized repentant sinners in water and told them of Another who would baptize in the Spirit. Except you are born of all that John's water baptism signified (REPENTANCE) and of all that Spirit baptism signifies (REGENERATION) you cannot enter the kingdom of God.

privileges which once had been his and the opportunities he had wasted. For, while being born of believing parents does not automatically confer a place in God's family it does greatly increase opportunity and responsibility.

b. Being born again has nothing to do with *fine intentions* for it is "not of the will of man" (John 1:13). There are multitudes who think that a place in heaven can be earned by human effort. In fact this false notion is at the root of all the false religious systems on earth. That kind of religion is nothing else but the expression of "the will of man" in spiritual matters while completely ignoring the will of God. God says, "By grace are you saved through faith; and that not of yourselves: it is the gift of God; not of works, lest any man should boast" (Ephesians 2:8, 9).

Nobody earns a place in God's family by following some religious scheme. Pilgrimages and penances, fasts and flagellations, rules and resolves cannot earn us salvation. It is "not of the will of man." No amount of human will power and determination can bring about the new birth. It is not a question of turning a new leaf but of taking a new life.

c. The new birth has nothing to do with *fleshly impulses* or human desire. It is "not of the will of the flesh." The desire to be a child of God does not make a person a child of God any more than the desire to be the son of a millionaire makes a person the son of a millionaire. The "will of the flesh" cannot cancel the "works of the flesh" and the Bible is clear on what these are. The Bible says, "Now the works of the flesh are these; Adultery, fornication, uncleanness, lasciviousness, idolatry, witchcraft, hatred, variance [quarreling], emulations [jealousy], wrath, strife, seditions [factions], heresies, envyings, murders, drunkenness, revelings, and such like . . . they which do such things shall not inherit the kingdom of God" (Galatians 5:19-21). Even when "the flesh" puts on its best behavior it is no better. In one place the apostle Paul lists all his religious assets as a man in the flesh, and then writes them off as a total liability. He calls the whole lot "useless rubbish" (Philippians 3:4-8). Human nature is human nature and can never be anything else no matter how much a person may desire to be different.

The apostle Paul says, "In me (that is, in my flesh) dwells no good thing: for to will is present with me; but how to perform that which is good, I find not" (Romans 7:18). God says that no flesh shall glory in His presence (1 Corinthians 1:29). The desire to be born again must be planted in the human soul by the Holy Spirit, not generated by some carnal means for some selfish reason.

2. Three Simple Conditions

We have seen three things which being born again is *not*. How it comes about is really very simple but also very sublime. You will notice that in John 1:12 there are three verbs. Putting them in their logical order they are:

➢ **Believe**

➢ **Receive**

➢ **Become**

In a natural birth there is a human agency and a divine agency. When the laws which bring about a physical birth are obeyed the result is a new life brought into being by man's cooperation with God. Man does his part; God imparts the life. Spiritual birth is like that too. We have a part to perform but God imparts the life. Let us see how it works.

a. The first thing is to *believe*; specifically we are to "believe on his name." His name, of course, is Jesus. When the angel was sent to Joseph to announce the virgin birth of Christ he said, "you shall call his name Jesus: for he shall save his people from their sins" (Matthew 1:21). The name "Jesus" simply means "Savior." He saves His people from their sins. Listen to Peter's words, "Neither is there salvation in any other: for there is none other name under heaven, given among men, whereby we must be saved" (Acts 4:12). You will remember, of course, that sin is at the root of our problem. On the cross of Calvary the Lord Jesus died to save us from our sins. "For Christ also has once suffered for sins, the Just for the unjust, that he might bring us to God" (1 Peter 3:18). We are to believe therefore that He can and will save us personally from our sins.

b. The second thing is to *receive* Him. It is not sufficient to give mental assent to divine truth. Just as a young woman receives a young man in marriage to be her husband, so we must receive the Lord Jesus personally into our lives to be our Savior. To believe is only one part of the transaction. For example, suppose someone were to offer you a check for $1,000. You might believe the offer to be genuine but until you actually put out your hand and receive it that gift would never be yours. You might believe that the Lord Jesus is *the* Savior, you might believe He is the *only* Savior. But have you made Him *your* Savior? Have you acted on your belief and deliberately asked Him to be your Savior from sin? Have you received Him?

c. When a person believes in the Lord Jesus as the One and only Savior and receives Jesus Christ personally into his life God says to that person, "*become* a child of God." The miracle takes place, eternal life is bestowed, the Holy Spirit takes up His residence in the human personality and that person is born again, born of God.

The Result

The new birth brings into the human personality a new quality of life. The humblest plant in the forest is greater than the highest mountain on earth because that plant has life, *vegetable* life. The smallest animal in the world is greater than the mightiest tree in the forest because that creature has something greater than vegetable life; it has *animal* life. The weakest child on earth is greater than the cleverest or strongest animal for it has something greater than animal life; it has *human* life. The poorest child of God, the weakest, most feeble Christian is greater than the most brilliant, gifted and influential unregenerate person on earth because that Christian has something greater than natural life; he has *spiritual* life.

Spiritual life is a precious gift from God. It is the life of God Himself planted into the human personality. It is eternal, undying, incorruptible life. But the analogy of a new birth holds true. When a baby is born into a human family, life is there with all its vast potential but the infant itself needs love and care, warmth and food. Similarly when a person is born again that person is a spiritual baby. He needs spiritual nourishment, protection, guidance and help. The Bible puts it this way, "Being born again, not of corruptible seed, but of incorruptible, by the word of God, which lives and abides for ever. . . . As newborn babes, desire the pure milk of the word, that you may grow thereby" (1 Peter 1:23; 2:2).

That is why this course has been written. Have you been born again? If so, this course is for you, to help you grow up in your spiritual life and become a mature, useful servant of God as well as an adult son of God. If you are not born again you can accept God's conditions right now—believe that Jesus took your place and died for you, receive the risen Lord Jesus as your very own Savior from sin and become a child of God.

2

BEING SURE OF HEAVEN

An elderly and not too sophisticated lady accepted Christ as her Savior in a church service. That night, soon after retiring to bed, she was assailed with doubts. Was it really true? Had it actually happened? Could she be sure she was saved? It seemed to her that the Devil himself was firing the questions. In her simplicity she decided that the Devil was under her bed so, opening her Bible at John 3:16 she put her finger on the verse, leaned over the bed and thrust the Bible under the overhanging sheets. "Here," she said, "read it for yourself!"

For all her lack of sophistication the elderly lady was right. Assurance of salvation:

➢ Resides in the Word of God

➢ Rests on the work of Christ

➢ Results from the witness of the Spirit

In this lesson we are going to examine these three great foundation stones of assurance.

The Word of God

"Faith comes by hearing, and hearing by the word of God" (Romans 10:17). It is the Bible alone which settles the questions which arise about the validity of our salvation. The first thing the Devil did when he tempted Eve in the garden of Eden was to disarm her of the only weapon he feared— the Word of God. To all his suggestions Eve ought only to have replied, "Thus saith the Lord," and his defeat would have been swift and sure. Instead she tried to fend off his attacks with her own rationalizations (Genesis 3). The Christian who doubts his salvation has, somewhere along the line, allowed his grip upon the Word of God to be slackened by Satan.

1. The Authorship of the Bible

We cannot have lasting assurance that we are born again if we are questioning the *authorship* of the Bible. It is because God is the ultimate Author that it speaks with such authority to the heart, mind, will and conscience.[3] Peter tells us "the prophecy came not in old time by the will of man: but holy men of God spoke as they were moved by the Holy Spirit" (2 Peter 1:21).

2. The Accuracy of the Bible

Lasting assurance of salvation is impossible if we are questioning the *accuracy* of the Bible. The supposed errors and contradictions in the Bible, long the plaything of the skeptic, vanish when patiently investigated. In regard to the New Testament, for example, those acknowledged scholars Westcott and Hort, state: "The proportion of words virtually accepted on all hands as raised above doubt is very great. . . . The amount of what can in *any sense be called substantial variation* is but a small fraction of the whole residuary variation, and can hardly form more than a thousandth part of the entire text."[4] Of these minute parts of the New Testament which show variation from one manuscript to another, a further leading authority says: "Not one affects an article of faith or a precept of duty which is not abundantly sustained by other and undoubted passages."[5]

The accuracy of the Bible is attested by the Lord Jesus Himself. He always treated the Bible as inspired, quoted from it, upheld its authority and bowed to its precepts. He said, "The scripture cannot be broken" (John 10:35). If we lack assurance of salvation we need only to see what the Scripture says and then rest in the knowledge that we are reading what God Himself has caused to be written.

3. The Acceptability of the Bible

We cannot have lasting assurance of salvation if we are challenging the *acceptability* of the Bible. The doctrines and demands of Scripture often clash with natural desires and human wisdom. We cannot hope for assurance if we are ignoring or defying some known, specific command of God. All Scripture is not only "given by inspiration of God" it is also "profitable for

---

[3] If you have honest doubts abut this we suggest you read *Is the Bible the Word of God?* by W. Graham Scroggie (published by Moody press, Chicago).

[4] B. F. Westcott and F. J. A. Hort, The New Testament in Greek, II, 2, as cited by Lewis S. Chafer, Systematic Theology (Dallas, 1947) I, 87.

[5] Philip Schaff, as cited by Chafer, I, 88.

doctrine, for reproof, for correction, for instruction in righteousness: that the man of God may be perfect, thoroughly equipped for all good works" (2 Timothy 3:16, 17).

Assurance of salvation comes through believing what God has said in His Word. As John says, "If we receive the witness of men, the witness of God is greater" (1 John 5:9). The Lord Himself gives us this assurance: "My sheep hear my voice, and I know them, and they follow me: and I give unto them eternal life; and they shall never perish, neither shall any man pluck them out of my hand. My Father, which gave them me, is greater than all; and no man is able to pluck them out of my Father's hand" (John 10:27-29). Many other Scriptures offer the same assurance. True, there are some warning passages in the Bible but these do not materially alter the fact that "the gift of God is eternal life through Jesus Christ our Lord" (Romans 6:23). Remember, "the gifts and calling of God are without repentance [irrevocable]" (Romans 11:29), that is, God does not give with one hand and take away with the other. One of the greatest passages in the New Testament on assurance is Romans 8. Read it, study it, memorize it. It begins with "no condemnation" and ends with "no separation."

The Work of Christ

"For God so loved the world, that he gave his only begotten Son, that whosoever believes in him should not perish, but have everlasting life" (John 3:16). This great salvation text draws our attention to the fact that salvation is centered in the person and work of the Lord Jesus Christ.

1. Salvation from Sin's Penalty

The first fact to remember is that *Christ died to save us from sin's penalty.* "Christ died for our sins according to the scriptures" (1 Corinthians 15:3). The many sacrifices of the Old Testament all illustrate the significance of the death of Christ. These sacrifices were commanded by God in Old Testament times. The Jews had to bring them to God's alter when conscious of sin or when desirous of worshipping. Two of these sacrifices are particularly helpful in depicting what happened at a place called Calvary where the Lord Jesus was crucified. These are *the burnt offering* and *the sin offering*. You can read about them in Leviticus chapters 1 and 4. In bringing either of these offerings, the sinner was identified with the sacrifice by placing His hands upon the animal to be offered. But there the similarity ended. *The sin offering* pictured in advance the substitutionary death of Christ; *the burnt offering* depicted the victorious life of Christ. The sin offering was for the sinner to accept, as God's provision for his sin; the burnt offering was for God to enjoy. In the case of the sin offering, all the vileness of the sinner was symbolically transferred to the animal substitute. In the case of the burnt offering, all the virtue of the substitute was transferred to the sinner.

Together, these two offerings illustrate what happens when a sinner accepts Christ as Substitute and Savior. Paul puts it this way: "We pray you in Christ's stead [as His personal representatives], be reconciled to God. For he has made him [Christ] to be sin for us—He who knew no sin; that we might be made the righteousness of God in him" (2 Corinthians 5:20, 21). So then, Christ died to save us from sin's penalty.

2. Salvation from Sin's Power

Further, *Christ lives to save us from sin's power*. The Lord Jesus is "declared to be the Son of God with power, according to the spirit of holiness, by the resurrection from the dead" (Romans 1:4). The life of victory for the believer over the evil tendencies in his own heart, is linked with his complete identification with Christ's death, burial and resurrection.

The Lord Jesus is really and truly alive. This is no mere myth or dry dogma. It is a glorious fact. Because He lives He is *praying for us*. "This man, because he continues ever, has an unchangeable priesthood. Wherefore he is able also to save them to the uttermost that come unto God by him, seeing he ever lives to make intercession for them" (Hebrews 7:25). When we are conscious of sin and failure we should confess it to Him for "if we confess our sins, He is faithful and just to forgive us our sins, and to cleanse us from all unrighteousness. If any man sin we have an advocate with the Father, Jesus Christ the righteous" (1 John 1:9; 2:1).

Because He lives, He is *present with us*. He says, "All power is given unto me in heaven and in earth. And, lo, I am with you always, even unto the end of the world" (Matthew 28:18, 20). Things may get beyond us but they cannot get beyond Him. We can turn to Him in every situation for He is present with us.

Because He lives, He is *personally in us*. It is a striking fact that the same indissoluble, mystical relationship which exists between God the Father and God the Son exists also between God and the humblest believer. Jesus said, "Believe me that I am in the Father, and the Father in me . . . because

I live, you shall live also. At that day you shall know that I am in my Father, and you in me, and I in you" (John 14:10-11, 19-20).

3. Salvation from Sin's Presence

Moreover, *Christ will return to save us from sin's presence*. Heaven is a prepared place for a prepared people. Both are being prepared now. Jesus said, "I go to prepare a place for you" (John 14:2). The experiences through which we pass as believers are designed to mature us so that our enjoyment of heaven may be complete. There is, of course, a *permanent* preparation for heaven which takes place when we initially trust Christ as Savior. Our sins have all been judged in the cross of Christ and, therefore, will not be remembered against us (Isaiah 53:5; Hebrews 10:17). "God will not payment twice demand, first at my Savior's pierced hand and then again at mine." But then there is a *progressive* preparation for heaven which continues throughout life. The permanent preparation relates to our *standing* before God which is perfect; the progressive preparation for heaven relates to our *state*, or condition, which is often imperfect and will continue to be so as long as we are in the body. At the Lord's return the process will be complete.[6] We shall be perfect people in a perfect place. The Lord's coming for us will remove us to a scene where sin cannot come. "Beloved, now are we the sons of God, and it does not yet appear what we shall be: but we know that, when he shall appear, we shall be like him; for we shall see him as he is" (1 John 3:2).

The Witness of the Spirit

Every true believer in the Lord Jesus has the Holy Spirit, the third Person of the triune Godhead, resident in his heart. Paul says, "If any man have not the Spirit of Christ, he is none of his" (Romans 8:9). A number of other Scriptures support this.

One reason why believers fail to enjoy conscious assurance of salvation is because they are grieving the Holy Spirit (Ephesians 4:30). Any conduct inconsistent with the holy character of the Spirit of God causes Him to grieve and be saddened. Grieve, incidentally, is a love word; we can only grieve someone who loves us. Loss of assurance of salvation is not loss of

---

6 The Bible does not support the idea of an in-between state between death and entrance into heaven. The question of sin and salvation is settled in this life (Matthew 9:6; Luke 16:19-31; Philippians 1:20-23; 2 Corinthians 5:6-8).

salvation itself, just the conscious enjoyment of that salvation. If this is your case, now would be a good time to ask the Lord what, in your life, is grieving His Spirit. Then confess it and forsake it, seeking the Lord's cleansing and the Spirit's filling (Ephesians 5:18, 19). See lesson five.

Three words summarize the process of assurance as it is ministered to us by the Holy Spirit—*facts*, *faith* and *feelings*. Three times the witness of the Spirit is mentioned in the New Testament and each of these occasions takes up one of these items.

1. The Holy Spirit and Facts

First the Holy Spirit witnesses *to* the believer and, in this case, He witnesses of certain *facts*. The writer of Hebrews says, "But this man [Christ], after he had offered one sacrifice for sins for ever, sat down on the right hand of God; from henceforth expecting till his enemies be made his footstool. For by one offering he has perfected for ever them that are sanctified. Whereof the Holy Ghost also is a witness to us: for after that he had said before, This is the covenant that I will make with them after those days, says the Lord, I will put my laws into their hearts, and in their minds will I write them; and their sins and iniquities will I remember no more" (Hebrews 10:12-17). Here the Spirit witnesses to the fact that Christ has suffered; to the fact that God has spoken; and to the fact that, for the believer, sin has gone.

2. The Holy Spirit and Faith

Moreover the Holy Spirit witnesses *in* the believer and, in this case, witnesses to the reality of his *faith*. John writes, "And it is the Spirit that bears witness, because the Spirit is truth. If we receive the witness of men, the witness of God is greater: for this is the witness of God which he has testified of his Son. He that believes on the Son of God has the witness in himself: he that believes not God has made him a liar; because he believes not the record that God gave of His Son. And this is the record, that God has given to us eternal life, and this life is in his Son" (1 John 5:6, 9-11). The Holy Spirit here witnesses to the reality of our faith because "believing" is the vital link that makes the Word of God and the work of Christ of personal benefit to the individual.

3. The Holy Spirit and Feelings

Finally, the Holy Spirit witnesses *with* the believer and, in this case, witnesses to *feelings*. Paul writes, "For you have not received the spirit of bondage again to fear; but you have received the Spirit of adoption, whereby we cry, Abba, Father. The Spirit himself bears witness with our spirit, that we are the children of God: and if children, then heirs; heirs of God, and joint-heirs with Christ; if so be that we suffer with him, that we may be also glorified together" (Romans 8:15-17). The feelings of joy, peace and love which well up in the redeemed heart express themselves in the cry "Abba! Father!" *Abba* is the cry of an infant (colloquially it would be, in today's terminology, "papa" or "daddy"). *Father* is the word of an adult son. The Lord Jesus used these identical words in Gethsemane to express His agony at the thought of Calvary, when His feelings could find no other mode of expression (Mark 14:36). The Holy Spirit bears witness with the spirit of the believer that he has the right to address God in the identical way the Lord Jesus addressed Him. What more could we want than that?

Assurance of salvation then rests not on human opinion but on the Word of God; not on human effort but on the work of Christ; not in human emotion but from the witness of the Spirit. The questions to ask then, are these: Am I *consistently reading* the Word of God? Am I *confidently resting* in the work of Christ? Am I *consciously rejoicing* in the witness of the Spirit? If so, I shall be a radiant, happy Christian whose testimony for Christ will act as a magnet for other people.

3

KEEPING IN TOUCH WITH GOD

George Müller was a spiritual giant, a man who knew God well. Many are the stories and legends which have clustered around his memory. His life-work was to build five great orphan houses on Ashley Down in Bristol, England, and to feed, clothe and educate thousands of boys and girls. His simple rule of life was to make his needs known to no one but God. Dr. Rendle Short, a well-known Bristol surgeon, tells us that in his father's day, agnosticism did not dare to rear its head in Bristol because of the life and testimony of George Müller.

It is said of Müller that once he was conducting a service and a baby began to cry. The mother arose to take the baby out but George Müller stayed her with a wave of his hand. "Sit down, mother," he said. "We'll ask the Lord to put the baby to sleep."

On another occasion, so the story goes, George Müller was on his way to Canada to keep an appointment he was sure was in God's will. As the ship which was bringing him from England entered the St. Lawrence River it ran into a heavy fog. George Müller went to see the captain, a Christian friend of his. "Tell me, Captain," he said, "will we arrive in time for my meeting?" The captain, looking out at the fog from the bridge, replied, "Not unless the weather clears at once." George Müller was a man who knew how to talk to God so he suggested that they pray. In simple terms he reminded the Lord of his appointment, of his assurance that the appointment had been made in the will of God; he then requested that the fog be removed. When he had finished, the captain was about to pray when he felt a hand on his arm. "Don't you pray, Captain," said George Müller. The captain looked up in astonishment. "Why not?" he exclaimed. "For two reasons," said George Müller. "In the first place you do not really believe God is going to take away the fog and in the second place it has already gone."

The great secret of George Müller's saintly life lay in the intimate way he kept in touch with God. He learned so to prize communion with God that he came to regard it as his highest duty and privilege. He used to say that his first duty of the day was to "get his soul happy in the Lord." He allowed nothing to trespass on the time he set apart daily for his "quiet time" with God.

There are three basic elements to an effective daily quiet time with God. These are:

➢ The Word of God
➢ The Word with God
➢ The Word for God

In this lesson we are going to study these and give some practical suggestions for making the most out of our daily time alone with the Lord. In the garden of Eden, before sin entered the world, God and man spent time together in the cool of the day (Genesis 3:8). The entrance of sin spoiled all that. As a Christian you will find that the world, the flesh and the Devil (see chapter 4) combine to rob you of the time you set apart for God. It must be defended at all costs. At the root of all loss of enthusiasm for the things of God is the abandonment of the daily quiet time.

The Word of God

The first element in a successful quiet time is the Word of God. It is through the Bible that God speaks to us. Whether as infants in Christ needing "the sincere [pure] milk of the word" (1 Peter 2:2) or as mature Christians able to handle the meat of the Word (1 Corinthians 3:2; Hebrews 5:12), God speaks to us from the pages of the Bible. It is on the Word of God that the soul is nourished (2 Peter 1:16-19).

The young believer is often at a loss to know how and where to begin. The Bible is a very large book and contains many things hard to be understood (2 Peter 3:15-16). There are rules for Bible interpretation, commonly called principles of hermeneutics. Obviously it is not practical to expect the new believer to be competent in piecing together correctly the various parts which go to make up the total revelation of God, nor to expect him to be skilled in applying hermeneutical laws. Therefore we are going to suggest a simple, devotional method of reading the Bible. Later, as you become more proficient in your knowledge of God's Word, you can begin to refine your

Bible reading. In the meantime, here is a simple method which has helped thousands to find food for their spiritual lives in a daily, consistent meditation upon the Bible.

First, make sure you have a Bible with good, readable type. If you wish to use a modern-language paraphrase do so as supplementary reading to your more literal translation (such as the King James or similar versions). Keep a notebook and a pen available and write down the thoughts you receive in your daily meditation. Remember, "writing makes an exact man." If you cannot write down your thoughts, it is because they are too vague and pointless to do you any good.

Decide where you are going to begin your daily, consecutive reading of Scripture. You might wish to begin with the Gospel of Matthew, the book of Acts or Paul's epistle to the Romans. If you can, read the book through from cover to cover at a single sitting. It will not take long and will give you a general idea of the tone and content of the book on which you will be meditating. For this reading a paraphrase would be quite acceptable.

In your daily devotions do not try to take on a whole chapter unless it is a short one. A paragraph or two would be quite adequate. Read the portion through once or twice, always beginning where you left off the day before. The practice of opening the Bible at random and picking out an isolated text here and there cannot be recommended. You would not read any other book that way so do not treat God's Book so arbitrarily.

Now that you have read the day's passage go back over it and, one by one, ask yourself the following questions, seeking the answers in the Scripture portion itself. Is there:

➤ Any sin for me to avoid?

➤ Any command for me to obey?

➤ Any promise for me to claim?

➤ Any lesson for me to learn?

➤ Any blessing for me to enjoy?

➤ Any victory for me to gain?

Is there any new thought:

➤ About the Father?

➤ About Jesus Christ the Son?

> ➢ About the Holy Spirit?
> ➢ About Satan?
> ➢ About man?

In summary:

> ➢ What is today's main thought?
> ➢ How can I apply this to my life?

By asking the questions of the passage in the first person you will be making the portion personally your own. Through prayer ask God the Holy Spirit to relate what you read to your own spiritual needs and to show you how to apply the lessons in your own life. You might like to use the language of the psalmist when he prayed, "Open thou mine eyes, that I may behold wondrous things out of thy law" (Psalm 119:18). Write down in your notebook the discoveries you make from the passage. Do not expect to find an answer to every question in each day's portion, but do expect to find some of the questions answered.

The Word with God

Having allowed God to speak to you from His Word, the next thing is to speak to God in prayer. This does not mean reciting to God some formal, written prayer. It means speaking to God in your own words just as you would speak to anyone else.

Prayer is the greatest privilege we have on earth. In some marvelous way not fully revealed to us, prayer is effective. It is one of the laws of the universe. God takes the prayers of His people into account when directing the course of events on earth (Revelations 8:1-6). We have direct access to God as believers (Hebrews 10:19-22) and need only the Lord Jesus to be our Mediator (1 Timothy 2:5).

The portion you have been reading from God's Word will, naturally, suggest a number of things to you about which to pray. It will suggest sins from which you need cleansing, commands you can obey only with the help of the Holy Spirit (see chapter 5), blessings you want God to make real in your experience. You will learn to take the matters about which God has been speaking to you and speak about them to God not only for yourself but for others.

1. Confession

There are a number of elements which make up prayer. There is *confession.* "If we say that we have no sin, we deceive ourselves, and the truth is not in us. If we confess our sins, he is faithful and just to forgive us our sins, and to cleanse us from all unrighteousness" (1 John 1:8-9). Sins are to be confessed directly to God. In one of his great penitential psalms, David put it like this: "Have mercy upon me, O God, according to your loving-kindness: according unto the multitude of your tender mercies blot out my transgressions. Wash me thoroughly from my iniquity, and cleanse me from my sin. For I acknowledge my transgressions: and my sin is ever before me. Against you, you only, have I sinned, and done this evil in your sight" (Psalm 51:1-4). We have a God who is "rich in mercy" (Ephesians 2:4). He promises to cleanse us for sin we confess to Him (1 John 1:7). When another person has been harmed or offended by our sin then it needs also to be confessed to that person and the wrong put right (Matthew 5:23-24).

2. Petition

Another aspect of prayer is the familiar one of *petition.* God wants us to ask Him for things and to share with Him our hopes and aspirations. "Ask and it shall be given you; seek, and you shall find; knock, and it shall be opened unto you" (Matthew 7:7). When asking things of God we should be specific and definite. We should, of course, ask according to His will (Matthew 26:39) and with a pure motive (James 4:3). We should present our petitions in the name of the Lord Jesus (John 16:23-24) and with hearts that have been cleansed of sin (Psalm 66:18; Matthew 5:23-24). Obviously we need help to pray in a way acceptable to God. This help has been provided for us in the Person of the Holy Spirit. Paul tells us that "the Spirit also helps our infirmities: for we know not what we should pray for as we ought: but the Spirit Himself makes intercession for us with groanings which cannot be uttered. And he that searches the hearts knows what is the mind of the Spirit, because he makes intercession for the saints[7] according to the will of God" (Romans 8:25-27). The word "helps" in this passage is interesting. The only other occasion of its use is found in Martha's plea to the Lord Jesus when, criticizing her sister Mary, she said, "Bid her therefore that she

---

[7] The word "saint" in New Testament usage is a general descriptive word for all Christians. The same Greek word *(hagios)* signifies "holy" which, of course, is an attribute of God and is a characteristic He expects of all Christians. (See for example 1 Corinthians 1:2).

help me" (Luke 10:40). She needed some practical, down-to-earth help. That is exactly the kind of help the Holy Spirit offers us in prayer.

3. Intercession

A similar aspect of prayer is *intercession.* Petition is asking for ourselves; intercession is asking for others. We have loved ones who are perhaps not yet Christians in the Bible sense of the word or friends who are straying away from God. We need to intercede for them. There are missionaries serving God in foreign countries and Christian leaders here at home. They need to be prayed for regularly. God's work is vast. It is one of our greatest privileges and responsibilities as Christians to have a share in this work by praying for those who are engaged in it. Many Christians keep a list of Christian workers for whom they wish to pray regularly. They keep in touch with them, learn their needs, their opportunities, their problems and then intercede for them. Paul knew the value of intercession. Study his prayers in the epistles he wrote in the New Testament. Look at some of the things for which he asked the Christians at Rome to pray (Romans 15:30-32). We are told to intercede for our country and for those in authority (1 Timothy 2:1-3). Truly, there is no excuse for wasting time when there is so much for which we need to pray.

4. Adoration

Another aspect of prayer is *adoration.* This is true worship, quietly waiting in God's presence, enjoying Him, being occupied with Himself and telling Him how worthy He is to receive our love and homage. Many of the psalms are taken up with this aspect of prayer. Adoration is the highest form of prayer. It is precious indeed to God and rare (John 4:23). It is illustrated in Mary's act of devotion when she broke her alabaster box of precious ointment so that the whole house was filled with its fragrance (John 12:3).

5. Thanksgiving

An important aspect of prayer is *thanksgiving.* When the Lord Jesus cleansed ten leapers He was grieved because only one of them returned to thank Him (Luke 17:17). One of the sins God counts in His indictment of the heathen is that they are not thankful (Romans 1:21). Examine this verse in its context and you will find the sin of ingratitude in very bad company indeed. Some Christians like to keep a record of (1) when they began to petition God for something or began to intercede for someone and (2) when the answer was given. Such a record could be useful in helping us remember to give thanks. In Old Testament times, the Jews were required to bring offerings and animal sacrifices to God in order to express their needs and their appreciation of Him. These requirements are a thing of the past. Our sacrifices are spiritual. We are instructed to "offer the sacrifice of praise to God continually, that is, the fruit of our lips giving thanks to his name" (Hebrews 13:15).

The Word for God

An important result of a daily quiet time with God is to share with others the good things God has bestowed upon us. If we have been blessed in our heart it will come out of our mouth (Matthew 12:34).

There are two major bodies of water in the land of Israel, one is the Sea of Galilee and the other is the Dead Sea. Both these lakes receive into their basins the waters of the River Jordan. The Sea of Galilee contains sweet, fresh water. It abounds with fish and its shores are fertile. The Dead Sea is acrid and bitter and nothing grows along its banks. The difference between the two streams is remarkable and the explanation simple. The Sea of Galilee receives the flowing water of Jordan and then passes it on below. The Dead Sea receives the water of Jordan but it has no outlet except by evaporation. What we receive from above in our daily quiet time with God we should pass on to others below. This will enable us to stay fresh in our spiritual lives.

There are so many needy people all around us. Ask the Lord to lead you to a relative or a friend who is not yet a true Christian or to a discouraged Christian or to a backslider. It could well be your joy today to say something, in the power of the Holy Spirit, which will be a great blessing spiritually to someone else. Do not be afraid to share your faith with someone else. Tell them how God has changed your life. Paul says, "God has not given us the spirit of fear; but of power, and of love, and of a sound mind" (2 Timothy 1:7).

But you may be tempted to say, "But I'm too shy. I'm always at a loss for words." Moses made the excuse, "O my Lord, I am not eloquent . . . but I am slow of speech, and of a slow tongue" (Exodus 4:10) when confronted with God's demand that he speak to Pharaoh. "I can't speak," said Moses. As a matter of fact he spoke far too much and, in the end, was kept out of the Promised Land because he "spoke unadvisedly with his lips" (Psalm 106:33; Numbers 20:9-13).

We can speak well enough about other things. Dr. Stephen Olford, a well-known Bible teacher, tells of an encounter he had on one occasion with a young man who complained of his inability to speak for Christ. Dr. Olford asked the young man if he had any hobbies. For five minutes the young man described, in glowing terms, his motorcycle and his interest in engines. Finally Dr. Olford stopped him. "Young man," he said, "when you spend as much time thinking about the Lord Jesus as you do thinking about your motorcycle you'll be able to talk about Him too."

4

KNOWING YOUR ENEMIES

Perhaps you remember the fairy story of Jack the Giant Killer. Jack was a puny tailor who liked to boast about his prowess as a warrior. The land in which he lived was infested by giants who terrorized the countryside. Jack liked to imagine that he could fight and slay them all. In his workshop, one hot summer's day, Jack was plagued by flies and sallied forth to do battle against them. He became adept at killing more than one of the flies at a single swipe of his hand. "Three at a single blow!" he boasted to a customer, "Three at a single blow!" The customer thought Jack was talking about giants and thus the little tailor was brought before the king and launched on his remarkable career as a giant slayer!

While we must take the story of Jack with due skepticism he does serve to introduce us to three very important and dangerous giants which confront the Christian at every step of his Christian life. These giants we must subdue, if we are to enter into the peace, joy and success which is God's will for every child of His. These giants are:

➢ The World—The External Foe

➢ The Flesh—The Internal Foe

➢ The Devil—The Infernal Foe

For our encouragement we can look upon them as having already been defeated by Christ. They are powerless to harm us so long as we face them on the ground of His mighty victory on the cross of Calvary.

Before assessing the strength, subtlety and strategy of these three foes let us remind ourselves of a very important Biblical truth regarding them. The Bible frequently sets against the world, the flesh and the Devil the three Persons of the Godhead, the Father, the Son and the Holy Spirit. We will cite one or two examples and suggest that you study the truth further for yourself in your own Bible study.

1. God the Father Opposes the World

Read, for example, that great intercessory prayer of the Lord Jesus recorded in John 17. Again and again the two words stand in contrast—the world, the Father. "O Father, glorify me with your own self with the glory which I had with you before the world was. I have manifested your name unto the men which you gave me out of the world. . . . I pray for them: I pray not for the world, but for them which you have given me: for they are yours" (John 17:5, 9). Remember, too, the sharp words of the apostle James, "You adulterers and adulteresses, know you not that the friendship of the world is enmity with God? whosoever therefore will be *a friend of the world is the enemy of God"* (James 4:4). In this verse, "God" is a reference to the Father (the other two members of the Godhead are mentioned in the wider context).

2. God the Spirit Opposes the Flesh

The great Adversary of the flesh is God the Holy Spirit. In one of the earliest references to the flesh in Scripture this truth is evident. God said to Noah, "My spirit shall not always strive with man, for that he also is flesh" (Genesis 6:3). The whole context of the statement is that of an utterly carnal and self-oriented society. The Lord Jesus contrasted the flesh and the Spirit in making known to Nicodemus the need for the new birth. He said, "That which is born of the flesh is flesh; and that which is born of the Spirit is spirit" (John 3:6). The Christian is told to "walk not after the flesh, but after the Spirit" (Romans 8:4) and, in a very strong statement, Paul states that *"the flesh lusts against the Spirit, and the Spirit against the flesh:* and these are contrary the one to the other" (Galatians 5:17).

3. God the Son Opposes the Devil

The Devil is opposed especially by God the Son. The very first promise and prophecy of Scripture brings into sharp opposition the seed of the woman (Christ) and the seed of the serpent (Satan). God says, "And I will put enmity between you and the woman, and between your seed and her seed; it shall bruise your head, and you shall bruise his heel" (Genesis 3:15). This is an oblique but nonetheless real reference to the consummation of a timeless conflict in the death of the Lord Jesus upon the cross of Calvary and His subsequent victory over Satan and all his hosts. The Lord Jesus was "in all points tempted like as we are, yet without sin" (Hebrews 4:15) but the actual record of that temptation (literally, "testing") is brought into focus in the confrontation between the Lord Jesus and the Devil in the wilderness (Matthew 4:1-11). The apostle John summarized the ministry of the Lord in these words: "For this purpose *the Son of God was manifested, that he might destroy the works of the devil"* (1 John 3:8).

It is evident, therefore, that three giants stalk the globe, fearful enemies of the human race. As we shall see, the Christian can learn to reckon them as defeated foes. The triune God has ranged Himself against our adversaries. We must now study our foes in more detail so that we might know how to take advantage of the sources of power at our disposal.

The World—The External Foe

1. The World Defined

When we think of the world, we tend to think of the planet Earth on which we were born. Sometimes the Bible refers to the world in this way too. But frequently, when the Bible refers to the world, it is referring to something quite different. It is referring to human life and society as it has been constituted since the entrance of sin into this sphere—human life and society with God left out. The world, in this technical, Biblical sense, is the Devil's lair for sinners and his lure for Christians. In this lesson, references to the world have to do with this state of affairs, not with the planet as such.

Our understanding of what the Bible means by the world will be aided if we consider one of the illustrations the Bible uses to depict it. Take, for example, the frequent references in the Old Testament to the land of Egypt, one of the greatest nations of antiquity and one which comes frequently into the Bible story. Egypt is a frequently used illustration of the world. In its splendor, its learning, its religion, its culture, its government, its pleasures, its history, its ambitions, its power, its needs, its ignorance of God, its attitudes, its deep-seated hatred of God's people, Egypt is a type, a picture, of the world. The very first mention of Egypt in the Bible sets the tone for subsequent references. It was a snare for Abraham's pilgrim feet. It drew him out of the path of obedience to God and dependence upon Him. It exerted a subtle influence upon Abraham so that he compromised his usefulness to God, failed miserably and ended up covered with confusion and shame (Genesis 12:10—13:4). Egypt is a perfect cameo of the world and is frequently introduced into the Bible story as such. Many other places, people, nations, incidents and things in the Old Testament are also of illustrative significance. The New Testament calls several of them "types" or pictures (1 Corinthians 10:11).

We have all been born into a world society which is antagonistic toward the things of God. This antagonism is often well disguised, but it is there just the same. There is much about human life and society which is splendid and attractive. There is much about the world that appears harmless or, at least, neutral. But it is still the implacable foe of God; He says so. It stands opposed to true spirituality, holiness and godliness. The world's methods, even when clothed in religious garb, are generally not God's methods. The world's horizons are dominated by the things of time and sense. It has no real sympathy with the things which are dear to God's heart. When He sent His Son to this planet, the world system arranged for His murder on the cross. Stripped of its religious guise, the world is opposed to everything Biblical.

2. The World Defeated

a. *In a Positional Sense.* Every Christian has been born again and has been given a change in his citizenship. Paul says, "Our conversation [the word is more correctly translated "citizenship"] is in heaven; from whence also we look for the Savior, the Lord Jesus Christ" (Philippians 3:20). The Christian's attitude to the world is well put by the apostle Paul in the words, "Now then we are ambassadors for Christ" (2 Corinthians 5:20). An ambassador lives in a foreign country but never forgets where his true citizenship is nor why he is in that alien land. He is there solely to represent his country and extend its interests. As ambassadors for Christ we are in the world but we are not of the world. We represent the interests of heaven in this present evil world in which we live. Our true interests are in the world to come.

b. *In a Practical Sense.* The world can put on a deceptive front. It has many allurements, many pleasures, many interests, many noble facets, all of them made stronger in their attraction for the Christian because of natural ties and because of past associations before conversion. The Christian must always remember, however, that the world is God's enemy. His attitude toward the world can be summed up in a single word—*separation.* "Be not unequally yoked together with unbelievers. . . . Come out from

among them and be separate, says the Lord" (2 Corinthians 6:14-
17). The Biblical doctrine of separation is not, as is mistakenly
believed by some, a doctrine of isolation. Many have tried to retire
from the world by seeking institutional seclusion. Unfortunately
the world is to be found there as much as anywhere else.
Separation does not mean withdrawing from normal social
contacts with men and women. The Lord Jesus deliberately
mixed with all classes of people in a normal, friendly way; in fact,
He was called "a friend of publicans and sinners" (Matthew
11:19). However, His contacts with people were always
redemptive in character. Separation, as a Biblical doctrine, has to
do with *insulation,* not *isolation.* The believer is to be a live
electrical wire, in touch at one end with the power and at the
other end with the need, but insulated by the Holy Spirit against
such contacts with the world as would short-circuit his usefulness.

The apostle Peter best illustrates, perhaps, what a Christian attitude
should be toward the world. He tells us we are to be strangers and pilgrims
(aliens) in this world (1 Peter 2:11). A stranger is a man away from home; a
pilgrim is a man going home. We are in the world but we are not of the
world.

The Flesh—The Internal Foe

1. The Character of the Flesh

The flesh is another of those words which have a double meaning in
Scripture. It is used, sometimes, in the ordinary sense of the flesh of the
body. It is frequently used, however, in a special, technical sense to depict
the desires and lusts which are so characteristic of human nature. Every
human being was born with King Self firmly seated on the throne of the
personality. The nature with which we were born can do nothing right in the
sight of God. Paul says, "I know that in me (that is in my flesh) dwelleth no
good thing" (Romans 7:18).

a. *Its Religious Aspect.* The flesh can be very *religious.* Paul says,
"I might also have confidence in the flesh. If any other man thinks
that he has whereof he might trust in the flesh, I more . . ."
(Philippians 3:4). He goes on to list eight things of a religious
nature which were once his confidence and his boast. He counted

these as "gain" and put them down on the asset side of the balance sheet of his life. When he met Christ, however, he realized that these things were all the products of the flesh and, therefore, far from being assets, were total spiritual liabilities. He says, "But what things were gain to me, those I counted loss for Christ" (Philippians 3:7). In fact he uses a particularly strong expression to describe these imagined religious assets. He calls them dung, or refuse (verse 8).

b. *Its Repulsive Aspect.* The flesh can also be very *repulsive.* Paul says, "Now the works of the flesh are these: Adultery, fornication, uncleanness, lasciviousness, idolatry, witchcraft, hatred, variance [quarreling], emulations [jealousy], wrath, strife, seditions [factions], heresies, envyings, murderers, drunkenness, revellings, and such like . . ." (Galatians 5:19-21). He says, "They that are after the flesh do mind the things of the flesh. . . . To be carnally minded is death . . . because the carnal mind is enmity against God: for it is not subject to the law of God, neither indeed can be. So then, they that are in the flesh cannot please God" (Romans 8:5-8).

2. The Conflict with the Flesh

The nature with which we were born can do nothing right, so far as God is concerned. That is why He insists on a new birth. The nature we receive when we are born again can do nothing wrong. This is what the apostle John means when he says, "Whosoever is born of God does not commit sin; for his seed is in him: and he cannot sin, because he is born of God" (1 John 3:9). That statement does not mean that a Christian cannot sin. Such a teaching is contrary both to experience and to Scripture as the apostle John would be the first to teach us (1 John 1:8-10). What John is saying is that the divine nature, implanted in the human personality at the time of the new birth, is incapable of sin. Peter says the same thing when he reminds us that we are born again "not of corruptible seed, but of incorruptible, by the word of God, which lives and abides for ever" (1 Peter 1:23).

It is evident, therefore, that the Christian has two natures. He has the original nature with which he was born and he has a new nature, a divine nature, imparted to him at the time of his new birth. These two natures are in constant conflict. Read carefully Romans chapter 7 and you will see that even the great apostle Paul was aware of this conflict. All too often the old nature with its lusts and passions, ambitions and desires, selfishness and sin wins out in the struggle. The old nature is very strong and often we feed it by the kind of book we read, the type of television program we watch and the sinful passions in which we indulge.

3. The Conquest Over the Flesh

a. *The Eternal Fact.* How can we obtain victory over the flesh? The Biblical answer is startling! Only by death! There are two aspects of this death which need to be grasped. First, there is what we might call the eternal fact of our death. Paul talks about this in Romans 6 where he says, "Knowing this, that our old man [the man of old, the man we used to be] is crucified with him. . . . He that is dead is freed from sin. . . . Likewise reckon you also yourselves to be dead indeed unto sin, but alive unto God through Jesus Christ our Lord." This is one of the most revolutionary concepts in the New Testament. When Christ died, I died. He died not only *for* me, but *as* me. In God's eternal counsels it was decreed that Christ's death upon the cross of Calvary should be my death. That is the eternal fact. It is something we must know, reckon to be true and believe. The very figure of the old man being crucified speaks volumes. Of all the deaths a suicide might choose there is one form of death he cannot inflict upon himself. He cannot crucify himself. The illustration of crucifixion shows that the Christian is not expected to put his old nature to death by his own efforts. This is impossible! Prolonged fasts and similar approaches to the problem of the flesh all miss the mark. The eternal fact is that God has already put the old nature to death at Calvary.

b. *The Daily Act.* God has dealt with the old nature but He expects the Christian to deal with it too. Our part is to appropriate what God has done. In Romans 6:6-13 Paul uses three words to show exactly how we appropriate in the daily act the eternal fact of our death with Christ. These words are *know*, *reckon* and *yield*. A simple illustration will help us understand what's involved.

A business man discovers that his payroll amounts to $5,000 but his bookkeeper tells him there is only $50 in the bank. He therefore goes to the bank and arranges for a $7,500 loan to be secured by a guarantor. He then tells the bookkeeper to make out the pay checks because there is now more than enough money to meet the payroll. But when the first workman comes in for his check the bookkeeper refuses to give it to him and points out to him the $50 balance in his books as being inadequate to meet a $5,000 payroll. What is wrong with the bookkeeper's explanation? He is failing to *reckon*. He is ignoring the fact that adequate provision has been made to cover every liability and, in so doing, he is acting foolishly and bringing dishonor on his employer.

Just so, the eternal fact is that God has made provision by the death of Christ for every possible temptation. The daily act is to know that fact to be true and to reckon on it in the moment of temptation. Yielding to the Holy Spirit is what makes it actually work in day to day experience.

Suppose, for instance, a new Christian has a habit of using foul language. He *knows* that such talk is contrary to God's will (Colossians 3:8) so he should *count himself dead* to such a practice. It is part of his old nature and, as such, has been put to death. Then, whenever the urge comes again he should *yield* to the Holy Spirit (either as a conscious or as a subconscious act) in the very moment of the temptation. Soon bad language will become repulsive to him. This is covered in more detail in chapter five.

The Devil

1. His Downfall

The Christian has one other foe. Some forty different names and titles are used in the Bible to describe him. We know him best as the Devil, or Satan. It would appear from Isaiah 14:12-17 and Ezekiel 28:11-19 that Satan was once an angelic being of the highest order, entrusted by God with the most exalted functions. From this lofty place of trust and privilege he fell because he conceived the idea of exalting himself above God. He was cast down from heaven along with a host of other angelic beings who followed him in his rebellion and is, today, the most implacable foe of the human race in general and of the Christian in particular.

2. His Dominions

Satan is a very powerful and brilliantly clever being but he does not have the attributes of deity. He is neither omnipotent, omniscient nor omnipresent. He makes up for this fatal deficiency as best he can by the thorough organization of his spiritual empire. Christians are told by Paul that they do not wrestle against flesh and blood but "against principalities, against powers, against the rulers of the darkness of this world, against spiritual wickedness in high places" (Ephesians 6:12). It would seem that, in the unseen spirit world, there are organized ranks of wicked spirits, arranged in some kind of hierarchy. Some of these evil beings are very powerful. Daniel learned that two of them could hold up Gabriel, the herald angel, for a period of three weeks and that Michael, the archangel, had to come to his assistance before Gabriel could finally deliver to Daniel the message with which he had been entrusted by God (Daniel 10:12-21).

Satan's demon hordes are very numerous and exceedingly malicious. Many of the miracles of the Lord Jesus were directed against demons which had caused numerous types of physical ailments in their human victims. The Lord cast a whole legion of demons out of one sufferer (Mark 5:1-20). In the Roman army a legion consisted of some six thousand men! There is every reason to believe that behind the present day resurgence of interest in spiritism, astrology, occultism, fortune-telling, secular prophecy and the like is the activity of demons (2 Timothy 3:1-7; 1 Timothy 4:1-3). Modern man scoffs at the existence of demons just as his ancestor would have scoffed at the existence of germs and viruses, had he been told they existed. The unbelief of men does not alter the fact that these beings exist and that they are the enemies of mankind.

Satan is given three principal titles in the Bible. He is called *"the prince of the power of the air"* (Ephesians 2:2) and as such he heads up the spiritual hosts of wickedness described above. He is called *"the prince of this world"* (John 12:31) and, in this role, he guides the destinies of the nations to make them conform to his own interests and plans. It is worth noting in this connection that the Lord Jesus did not dispute Satan's claim to have the kingdoms of this world at his disposal (Luke 4:5-6). He is also called *"the god of this world"* (2 Corinthians 4:3-4) and, as such, blinds the minds of men to the truth of the gospel. He is a deceiver and a murderer (John 8:44). His chief activity at present seems to be that of deluding men into all kinds of false religious belief. For Satan's supreme desire is to be worshipped, preferably openly, but by deception if by no other way (2 Thessalonians 2:1-12).

3. His Defeat

We can be thankful that the Devil is no match for God. The key to victory over this powerful adversary is in submission to God. James tells us,

"Submit yourselves therefore unto God. Resist the devil, and he will flee from you" (James 4:7). The Lord Jesus defeated Satan by countering all his suggestions with the Word of God (Matthew 4:1-11). We have the same mighty weapon in our hands (2 Corinthians 10:4; Hebrews 4:12). In fact Christians have been provided with a complete set of spiritual armor, not only to enable them to withstand Satan's attacks but also to enable them to carry the warfare into Satan's territory (Ephesians 6:11-18). Be sure to look up these references and study them.

5

SUBMITTING TO THE SPIRIT

As you have been studying these lessons you have no doubt come to the conclusion that living the Christian life is a tall order. In fact, it is impossible! And, you are quite right. The only Person who can live the Christian life is Christ Himself. It is for this reason that, just prior to His departure from this earth, He promised to send another "Comforter," the Holy Spirit of God. It is the work of the Holy Spirit to make the Christian life a reality in the experience of the individual believer.

The name "Comforter" is an interesting one. The word the Lord Jesus actually used to describe the Holy Spirit was the Greek word *parakletos* which literally means "One called alongside to help" (John 14:16). For example, in connection with a Christian's prayer life Paul tells us that the Holy Spirit "helps our infirmities." He helps us to pray in accordance with the mind and will of God. The Greek word used in this case in the original text is only used in one other place in the New Testament. Consider the occasion in the life of the Lord Jesus when He was visiting the home of Lazarus, Mary and Martha in Bethany. Martha was busy possibly in the kitchen preparing a meal for the Lord and she became very annoyed because Mary, instead of helping her, chose rather to sit at Jesus' feet and listen to His conversation. Martha came bustling in at last and blurted out, "Lord, do you not care that my sister has left me to serve alone? bid her therefore that she help me" (Luke 10:40). It is the same word for "help" used in Romans 8:26 to describe the kind of help the Holy Spirit gives us when we pray. It is the same kind of help Martha wanted in the kitchen—practical, down-to-earth help right where we are and where we need it most.

There are three relationships the Holy Spirit sustains toward the world of lost, unsaved men and women. In this sphere He carries on:

> ➤ A Reproving Ministry
> ➤ A Regenerating Ministry
> ➤ A Restraining Ministry

First let us consider His *reproving* ministry. The Lord Jesus said, "When he is come, he will reprove the world of sin, and of righteousness, and of judgment" (John 16:8). He convicts men and women of the nature of sin, of the need for righteousness and of the nearness of judgment. He also carries on a *regenerating* ministry. The Lord told Nicodemus, "Except a man be born of water and of the spirit, he cannot enter into the Kingdom of God" (John 3:5). It is the Holy Spirit who imparts the life of God to the human spirit when a person accepts the Lord Jesus as personal Savior. Moreover, He carries on a *restraining* ministry. We are told that one of His great functions in the world today is to "hinder" the development of the "mystery of iniquity" (2 Thessalonians 2:7). Until God permits otherwise, the floodtides of human wickedness are kept in check. Again and again during the long ages of human history, God has visited men with spiritual awakenings which have defused the warhead of human ungodliness.

In this lesson we are concerned with the ministry of the Holy Spirit to the Christian. There are seven aspects, most of which we will only mention in passing since it is with the filling of the Spirit that we wish mostly to be concerned.

The Baptism of the Spirit

The baptism of the Spirit is mentioned only seven times in the New Testament—Matthew 3:11; Mark 1:8; Luke 3:16; John 1:26, 33; Acts 1:5; Acts 11:16 and 1 Corinthians 12:13. Look up these references in your Bible. You will observe that the first four references all have to do with the ministry of John the Baptist who told his Jewish listeners that he baptized people with water but, the coming Messiah would baptize people with the Holy Spirit. These four references, like the fifth one, are all prophetic in nature. In Acts 1:5 the Lord Jesus told the disciples that they would be baptized with the Holy Spirit "not many days hence." The baptism took place on the day of Pentecost just ten days after the Lord had made this promise. (Read Acts 2.)

The next reference to the baptism of the Spirit is historical. Peter, you may recall, had been directed by the Holy Spirit to leave Jerusalem and go to the Gentile city of Caesarea, there to meet with a group of devout Gentiles and preach the gospel to them. The result was that the door of the church[9] was opened to the Gentiles who were baptized with the Holy Spirit. The significance of this second baptism lay in the fact that the Jews scorned the Gentiles (John 4:9; Acts 10:28). It was necessary that the Jews be given an adequate sign that, in the church, there was to be no difference between Jew and Gentile. When Peter told his critics in Jerusalem what had happened they refrained from further comment. The baptism of the Gentiles by the Holy Spirit silenced their criticism as God intended it should.

The last reference to the baptism of the Spirit is doctrinal. Paul says, "For by one Spirit are we all baptized into one body, whether we be Jews or Gentiles, whether we be bond or free; and have been all made to drink into one Spirit" (1 Corinthians 12:13). In other words, it is by the baptizing work of the Holy Spirit that individual believers in the Lord Jesus become members of His mystical body, the church. This is the significance of the baptism of the Spirit. It is that work of the Holy Spirit which unites believers in a living union with the Lord Jesus as the Head of the church and one to another as equally important members of that church.[8] Every true believer is baptized thus by the Holy Spirit. Notice the use of the past tense and the use of the word "all" in this last direct scriptural reference to the baptism.

The Gift of the Spirit

On the day of Pentecost, the apostle Peter preached to thousands of Jews gathered in Jerusalem from all parts of the Roman world. The Holy Spirit convicted his hearers of their sin in crucifying the Lord Jesus Christ. When they asked Peter what to do he told them to repent, express their conversion in Christian baptism and they could be assured that they would receive the gift of the Holy Spirit (Acts 2:38). Every true believer has received this gift. Paul plainly states that "if any man have not the Spirit of Christ, he is none of his" (Romans 8:9). In other words, a person either is saved and consequently has received the gift of the Holy Spirit, or else he has never received the gift of the Holy Spirit because he is not saved.

---

[8] There are two uses of the word "church" in the New Testament. It is used to describe (1) a group of Christians meeting together in a given locality on a regular basis, and (2) all Christians everywhere regardless of the names they may have adopted to describe themselves.

Now the Holy Spirit is a Person, the third Person of the Godhead to be precise. Since He is a Person, He cannot be received by installments. For example, when a man accepts a woman into his life to be his wife, he receives the woman in her entirety and totality. Obviously, he does not always know all that he is receiving when he accepts her as his wife! Marriage is largely the process of discovering all that was really received on the wedding day. Just so, no Christian fully comprehends all that is involved when, at the moment of conversion, he is given the Person of the Holy Spirit to share his life. The Christian life is largely a matter of adjusting to the presence of God the Holy Spirit in the life and of constantly discovering new potential in Him.

Study the names given to the Spirit of God in the New Testament. He is the Spirit of truth (John 14:17); of faith (2 Corinthians 4:13); of grace (Hebrews 10:29); of holiness (Romans 1:4); of wisdom (Ephesians 1:17); of power, love and a sound mind—or discipline as some versions render this last word (2 Timothy 1:7); of life (Romans 8:2) and of glory (1Peter 4:14). All these things characterized the Lord Jesus when He lived on earth as can be seen from the most casual reading of the four Gospels. These things are to characterize us as we live our lives as Christians. The gift of the Spirit of God alone makes it possible for these traits of the character of the Lord Jesus to be reproduced in us.

The Indwelling of the Spirit

The Lord Jesus promised the Holy Spirit would be with the Christian for ever (John 14:16) and would be in Him (John 14:17). Paul challenged the Corinthian Christians with the awe-inspiring truth that the believer's body has become the temple of the Holy Spirit (1 Corinthians 6:19). The significance of this can be seen in the Lord's attitude toward the Temple in Jerusalem. Twice He cleansed that Temple, once at the beginning of His ministry and once again at the end (John 2:13-17; Matthew 21:12-13). That Temple again being defiled, He foretold its complete destruction (Matthew 24:1-2). It is a solemn thing to be a Christian and to have the Holy Spirit make one's body His Temple. To persistently and deliberately defile that Temple is to invite the destruction of it. Paul warns, "If any man defile the temple of God, him shall God destroy: for the temple of God is holy, which temple you are" (1 Corinthians 3:16-17). While this latter reference is taken by some to refer to the collective body of believers, such Scriptures as 1 Corinthians 5:1-5; 11:28-31 corroborate the truth that God is not to be mocked by a Christian's misconduct. The pulling down of the temple of the body can be done by sickness or by premature death.

The Seal of the Spirit

Paul tells us that the Holy Spirit is given to the Christian as the seal of God's redemption. When we trust in Christ for salvation, God seals us with His Holy Spirit (Ephesians 1:12-13). The idea behind a seal is that of a finished transaction. In many counties, when a legal contract is drawn up between two parties, the document is first signed, then sealed with a legal seal. The seal is the finishing touch to the transaction which confirms that the terms of the agreement are legal and binding on all parties.

There is a sense in which salvation is a legal contract between God and a human soul. In His Word, God sets forth the terms and conditions under which He will save a soul and guarantee to that one a full and free salvation. His name is on the contract as is evident from such Scriptures as Matthew 1:21; Acts 4:12; Romans 10:13. When a person becomes acquainted with God's terms of salvation and personally accepts those terms by receiving Christ as Savior, then he too becomes a party to the contract. God seals the transaction by putting the seal of His Spirit upon the believing Christian. While we, as Christians may and do fail, God cannot fail. Since the terms of the contract put the obligation for saving and keeping on God, we can rest secure in the salvation God has provided. This does not lead to looseness of life—the truth of the indwelling of the Spirit is guarantee against that.

The Earnest of the Spirit

Paul tells us that the Holy Spirit is not only God's seal upon the life of the Christian but He is also "the earnest of our inheritance until the redemption of the purchased possession, unto the praise of his glory" (Ephesians 1:14). The word "earnest" is not common in modern speech. There is one connection, however, where it is still used. In some countries, for example, if a person decides to make an offer for a house, the real estate agent will require that the would-be purchaser put down what is called "earnest money." He must make a deposit on the house, with his offer, in order to prove to the seller that he is in earnest about completing the transaction. In other words, the earnest money shows that the purchaser is serious about the offer and means business. Just so, the Holy Spirit has been given to the believer by God as proof that He is in earnest about the matter of salvation and that He means business when He promises to take the believer to heaven and give him an eternal inheritance. How great that inheritance is can be inferred from the character of the earnest—none other than God's Holy Spirit Himself!

The Anointing of the Spirit

All the above ministries of the Spirit are sovereign acts of God and are imparted impartially to all Christians when they accept Christ as personal Savior. There are two other works of the Spirit to be considered. One of these is the filling; the other is the anointing which some believe to be as unconditional as the others we have considered. The anointing is sometimes called "the unction" (1 John 2:20).

In Old Testament times prophets, priests and kings were given a special anointing for their work. The Lord Jesus received a special anointing of the Holy Spirit (Luke 4:18-19) before He began His public ministry. A study of the anointing of the Lord Jesus will show that He knew where to open God's Word and when to close God's Word in His dealings with men. In fact, He once closed it in the middle of a sentence, something which has a deep significance. (See verse 20.) From John's reference to the unction, it would seem that the anointing of the Spirit is in some way related to the proper use of the Scripture in Christian service. The Holy Spirit gives insight into the Word so that the taught Christian can, in turn, use the Word of God in an effective way when dealing with others. Hebrews 4:12 makes it clear that it is God's Word which speaks to men.

The Filling of the Spirit

1. The Practice of the Spirit-filled Life

Be sure to read carefully Ephesians 5:18-19. Paul tells us that we are not to be drunk with wine but we are to be filled with the Spirit. The verb he uses is in the present continuous tense and could be translated "be ye being filled." In other words, the filling of the Spirit is not a once-for-all experience but is something which needs to be continually repeated. Nor is it a sovereign, unconditional gift of God but, on the contrary, is the one ministry of the Spirit which depends, to a large extent, upon the cooperation of the Christian.

The illustration of being drunk is startling and significant. When a person becomes drunk he deliberately hands himself over to a filling with an alcoholic spirit. Under the influence of that spirit he is diabolically transformed. Often his character is radically changed so that his tongue is loosed or his temper is aroused or his tears flow, as the case may be. That he is drunk is evident in his walk and in his talk. But the next morning he is likely to be sober and will require a fresh intoxication if he is to show the effects of drunkenness again.

A person who is filled with the Spirit of God is Divinely transformed. His nature and his personality reflect the character of the Lord Jesus Christ. It is evident in his walk and in his talk. The Christian life is not a matter of our trying to imitate Christ; it is a matter of the Holy Spirit filling the life and making us like Christ. The filling is conditional however for the Holy Spirit can be grieved by our sin and disobedience (Ephesians 4:30). When this happens we need to confess our failure to the Lord, ask for cleansing and request a fresh filling of the Spirit. The Holy Spirit is grieved by anything in the Christian's life which is contrary to the known mind and will of God.

2. The Process of the Spirit-filled Life

How does a person become filled with the Spirit? *First, examine Colossians 3:16 and Ephesians 5:18-19.* Look these verses up in your Bible right now. Observe that the results of a life filled with the Word of God can be equated in some measure with the results of a life filled with the Spirit. Now picture an equilateral triangle marked as follows:

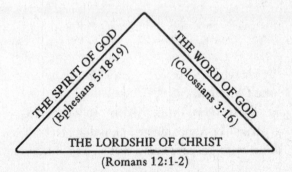

(Romans 12:1-2)

You begin by determining before God that Jesus is to be Lord, i.e., to be obeyed in your life in all things (Acts 2:36; 9:5; 16:6-10; James 4:15). Therefore in prayer tell God the Holy Spirit that you acknowledge His right to control your life (Romans 12:1-2). All impressions we receive and all impulses we express are through the channel of the body and the senses. The yielding of the body to the Holy Spirit is therefore a key requirement.

Having determined that Jesus is to be Lord in your life you begin to read the Word of God in a new way in your daily quiet time (see chapter 3) expecting God to speak to you as you read. As you thus read God's Word, the Spirit of God speaks to you and shows you things in your life which need to be given up or things which need to be said or done. Because Jesus has become your Lord, you yield to the authority of the Word of God, determined that you are going to obey. Many people have trouble at this point because they are afraid to trust God fully. Perhaps they feel that God is not fully dependable or fear that His commands might be capricious, arbitrary or too difficult to obey. God assures us that His will is good and perfect and acceptable (Romans 12:2) and that He Himself is utterly dependable (Romans 4:20-23). Moreover He will never ask us to do things for which He does not give the needed grace and power (2 Corinthians 12:8-10). Settle these facts firmly in your mind. Then, as you give in to God the Spirit of God will fill you and enable you to do what God says. This process is repeated continually, day after day as long as the Lord leaves you here on earth.

The Spirit-filled life is simply a life that is empty of self and yielded to the leading and the enabling of God's indwelling Spirit. The more you yield, the more He fills and the greater becomes your capacity for the things of God. This process is not a drudgery; it is a delight. As the Spirit of God makes the Word of God a living part of your life you will be filled with song. You will praise God again and again for who He is and for His wisdom, love and power. Moreover you will begin to reach out to other people in active efforts to win them to Christ. People will see Christ in you and will be attracted to Him.

3. The Precaution of the Spirit-filled Life

Supposing you fail. Does this mean that the whole process needs to be begun all over again? Perhaps an illustration will help. A friend who is an avid collector of antique books visits your home and notices on your shelf an old book which has been there for years gathering dust. He expresses an interest in the book so you give it to him, handling it carefully because many of the pages are loose. He accepts your gift and promises to take good care of it. A few days later you are cleaning up the bookshelf and you notice some pages which evidently had fallen out of the antique book. Now what do you do? Do you start all over again and re-present the book to your friend? Of course not! You simply give him the missing pages and explain that you had come across them since you gave him the book at his last visit. The loose pages were really all part of the original gift.

It is the same with the filling of the Spirit of God. As you see fresh areas of your life which are unsurrendered you simply hand those over to the Holy Spirit too. They were all part of the original yielding.

4. The Proofs of the Spirit-filled Life

The results of the fullness of the Spirit will be quite evident in a radiant and joyful life (Ephesians 5:19) and in an effective testimony for the Lord Jesus (Acts 8:17-22; 6:3, 5, 8-10; 13:52-14:1). It is the filling of the Spirit which makes the Christian life worthwhile and which, indeed, makes it possible at all.

6

SHARING YOUR FAITH

In A.D. 33 Jesus of Nazareth was hung upon a Roman cross on a hill near Jerusalem and left there to die. His enemies gathered around to deride Him; His friends, for the most part, forsook Him and fled. He died in agony and blood, alone.

1. The Miracle

Fifty years have come and gone and this same Jesus is worshipped as God in every major city of the Roman Empire. Hundreds of thousands of people confess Him as Savior and Lord and are willing to dare the most dreadful deaths to spread their faith.

Behind this miracle is the story of men and women who came into a living contact with the risen Christ. Their transformed lives, their radiant testimonies, their total commitment, their unshakable convictions turned the world upside down (Acts 17:6). Leading the way was the great apostle Paul.

2. The Motivation

In his famous letter to the Roman church, Paul tells what it was that motivated him in his deathless determination to tell others about his glorious Lord. He says, "I am debtor both to the Greeks, and to the Barbarians; both to the wise, and to the unwise." It made little difference to Paul whether a man was cultured or crude, an intellectual or a dunce. He would talk of Christ with equal passion to a runway slave like Onesimus or to a haughty member of the aristocracy like King Agrippa. We who know the truth in Christ are debtors to all mankind. We are like those lepers of old who, having stumbled on vast resources when their fellows were starving, said one to another, "We do not well; this day is a day of good tidings, and we hold our peace" (2 Kings 7:9).

Paul says, "As much as in me is, I am ready to preach the gospel to you that are at Rome also." The world was his parish. When Paul preached the gospel at Jerusalem, the religious centre of the world, he was mobbed; when he preached it at Athens the world's cultural centre, he was mocked; when, at last, he preached it at Rome, the world's political centre, he was martyred. It made no difference to Paul. He was bold to preach Christ beneath the very nose of Nero!

He says, "I am not ashamed of the gospel of Christ: for it is the power of God unto salvation to every one that believeth" (Romans 1:16). Paul knew the gospel to be the answer to the needs of men. Paul was no illiterate. He was a cosmopolitan man with a world vision, a liberal education, a wide range of interests and great intellectual power. He was well versed in the ways of the world and was outstandingly successful in telling others about Jesus Christ. He knew the power of the gospel.

The world's greatest need is not a better system of education, more social reform or new religious ideas. The world's greatest need is the gospel. The gospel message grips the mind, stabs the conscience, warms the heart, saves the soul and sanctifies the life. When people accept Christ as Savior their lives are transformed. Drunken men are made sober, crooked men are made straight, profligate women are made pure.

There is such a thing as criminal negligence. If a person were to see a house on fire and do nothing to arouse the occupants he would be guilty of criminal negligence. If a person were to see a child wandering out onto a busy street and do nothing to remove the child to safety he would be guilty of criminal negligence. For a Christian to see a neighbor, a friend, a workmate, a relative hurrying on to a Christless eternity and to do nothing to warn him makes him guilty of criminal negligence. Paul, in his last message to his friends from Ephesus could say, "I am pure from the blood of all men" (Acts 20:26). Read the whole passage, Acts 20:17-38. It is a tremendously important revelation on Christian responsibility.

A person can be motivated to action in several ways—from:

➢ A Sense of Discipline
➢ A Sense of Duty
➢ A Sense of Devotion

Discipline says, "I have to do it"; *duty* says, "I ought to do it," but *devotion* says, "I love to do it." The Christian can tell others about Christ under the compulsion of any of these motives. It is demanded of us; it is our duty. Paul says, "Woe is unto me if I preach not the gospel" (1 Corinthians 9:16). But the highest motive for telling others about Christ is surely the love motive. Paul could say "the love of Christ constraineth us" (2 Corinthians 5:14). We love the Lord Jesus so much that we cannot help but speak about Him to others. When a young woman falls in love with a young man she wants everyone to know about it. She talks to anyone who will listen about the wonderful person who has come into her life. This is the compulsion of love. This is what should really motivate us to tell others about the Lord Jesus. We love Him! And what joy comes flooding into our hearts when someone to whom we speak accepts Christ!

3. The Mandate

There are several prerequisites. First, and obviously, a person needs to be saved himself before he can point others to Christ. There is nothing more pathetic than to see an unsaved minister in the pulpit, or to see one lost sinner seeking to impart religious instruction to another. In the expressive language of the Lord Jesus, they are "blind leaders of the blind. And if the blind lead the blind, both shall fall into the ditch" (Matthew 15:14). Next, a Christian needs to be living a godly, consistent life for unbelievers are quick to detect hypocrisy and unreality. Then, too, those who would effectively share their faith need a thorough working knowledge of the Bible so that they can confront people, not with their own opinions, but with what God says. Finally a knowledge of people and their problems is needed and a willingness to be guided by the Lord. This lesson will serve simply as an introduction to the divine art of pointing others to the Savior.

The Approach

There are countless ways of making the contact which leads to a meaningful presentation of the claims of Christ. Much depends on the personalities involved, the circumstances and the Lord's leading. Here we will suggest various common methods of making the approach.

1. The Casual Approach

The casual approach is used, for example, when you meet someone on a train or in a waiting room and, after some generalities of conversation you steer the subject around to spiritual things. You might ask, "How relevant do you think the Bible is for today?" or "Did you know that the Bible has a great deal to say about the future of Russia?" or "What do you think of Billy Graham?" or some similar opening question. The idea then is led more directly to a discussion of one's personal relationship to the Lord Jesus.

2. The Curt Approach

The curt approach is employed when the question of salvation is broached abruptly and without any prior preparation. One fruitful Christian frequently uses this approach. One time, on a plane taking off on a flight, he leaned across to the lady next to him and said, "Madam, have you ever flown before?" When she said that she had not, he pointed out that take-off was, in many ways, the most dangerous part of the flight. He followed up with the comment, "If this plane were to cash where would you go? to heaven or to hell?" Such tactics can be used only by people with the right kind of personality and, unless used with an obvious and genuine regard for the other person's well-being, can be most offensive. This particular personal worker has an unusually attractive personality and, having been saved himself out of a life of deep enslavement to sin, has a genuine, almost transparently honest concern for those he meets.

3. The Comradely Approach

In this approach the ground is prepared beforehand by the forging of genuine links of friendship with people. These "redemptive friendships" can be very profitable. There are no end of ways in which comradeship can be shown. Deeds of kindness can be done, helpful visits can be made in times of stress or need, hospitality can be extended, mutual interests can be cultivated. Thousands of people have been won to Christ because someone took a friendly interest in them and invited them fishing, or for a game of golf or gave a helping hand shoveling snow or painting a room or sewing a dress. The friendship in such cases must be genuine and not merely sugar coating for a gospel pill.

4. The Canvass Approach

The canvass approach is frequently used by some cults but it is nonetheless productive for all that. In this approach a person goes from door to door selling Christian books or taking a religious poll with the deliberate intention of finding people willing to talk about spiritual things. Not everyone can do this sort of thing. Those who do engage in it have found it highly productive. Of course a philosophical attitude needs to be developed in order to take the snubs which will inevitably be met at some doors. Also an alert mind is needed for it is impossible to say what kind of a person will answer the door. Where a useful contact is made, often arrangements can be made for a further call or even for regular Bible study in the home.

5. The Correspondence Approach

Some people have carried on extensive correspondence with others by mail in order to win them to Christ. Pen pals have been deliberately sought for this purpose. Friends and relatives have been exposed to the gospel in this way. One danger lies in becoming pedantic and sermonic so that it is obvious that the only purpose of the correspondence is to preach. Also if letters become too long they become boring, especially if the handwriting is illegible. One good idea is to keep a supply of well-written and attractively produced tracts and booklets to insert in correspondence. Often people have been made to think seriously about spiritual things because they have been impressed by a good gospel leaflet. These are available from a number of Christian publishing houses. Thousands of people have been won to Christ by studying correspondence courses given to them or recommended to them by Christian friends. Write or call ECS Ministries to find out which courses are available and have been written especially for the non-Christian.

6. The Consultation Approach

This approach has been very successful. After an evangelistic service there are usually people who become concerned and who would value further private discussion about the issues of salvation. These conferences can be arranged immediately or a fixed appointment can be made at which time the plan of salvation can be explained more fully and the contact's particular problem faced.

7. The Cultural Approach

People from similar ethnic or religious backgrounds have much in common and can often be approached along that line. Foreign students in this country are often lonely and would welcome opportunities to visit in a home. Frequently they are genuinely interested in Christianity and would like to know more of its doctrines so that they can compare them with those of their own religion.

These are some of the approaches which can be used. Obviously there are many more. Each person should find the one which suits him best. Or, perhaps he could use several approaches. The important thing is to be available to the Lord and willing to respond as He leads.

The Appraisal

People who like to fish spend much time studying their sport. They have to know about the habits of the various kinds of fish and the environs where they are to be caught. They must study about lines and lures and bait. The Lord surely had this in mind when He said to Peter and Andrew, "Follow me, and I will make you fishers of men" (Matthew 4:19). No two people are alike. It is necessary to study the various kinds of people and to decide how to deal with a particular person once the approach has been made. Obviously we cannot discuss every type of person for each one is an individual with his own particular personality, background, problems, ideas and needs. However, as an introduction to the subject we might consider four different general categories into which unsaved people fall.

1. The Defiant Person

This is the person who is antagonistic to the gospel and to everything religious. He may be an atheist, an agnostic, a communist, a radical or even someone who has been brought up with a religious background but who has soured on the whole thing. This person will probably deny any belief in the Bible as the Word of God. Argument is generally useless, for the root cause of atheism goes far deeper than the professed rationalizing with which it is masked. The Bible teaches that the basic cause is a corrupt nature which loves sin (Psalm 14:1-3). The real problem is not in the intellect, but in the will. It is not that a person *cannot* believe in God but that he *will not* believe in God. The person who falls into this category needs to be confronted with God's Word regardless of his professed disbelief in it. A person may claim not to believe in the usefulness of inoculation against smallpox. His disbelief does not alter the fact that immunization works. The Bible says that "the word of God is quick [living], and powerful, and sharper than any two-edged sword, piercing even to the dividing asunder of soul and spirit, and of the joints and marrow, and is a discerner of the thoughts and intents of the heart. Neither is there any creature that is not manifest in his sight: but all things are naked and opened unto the eyes of him with whom we have to do" (Hebrews 4:12-13). It is not our intellectual cleverness which brings men to Christ but the Holy Spirit who convicts them of their need. To do this He uses His Word. Many a rabid unbeliever has been brought to the Savior's feet when God's Word has done its work of conviction in his soul.

2. The Disinterested Person

This person is not actively hostile to the gospel; he is simply not interested in it. The "god of this world" (Satan) has blinded him to spiritual reality (2 Corinthians 4:3-4). He is so taken up with this world, its problems and pleasures, its politics and personalities that he has no time for God, salvation or eternity. Here again it is the Word of God which brings conviction. Sin is a terrible reality in the human soul. It deadens. Paul says to the Ephesian Christians that they, in their unconverted days, were "dead in trespasses and sins: wherein you walked according to the course of this world, according to the prince of the power of the air, the spirit that now works in the children of disobedience . . . fulfilling the desires of the flesh and of the mind; and were by nature children of wrath" (Ephesians 2:1-3). God's Word awakens the sinner to his peril and to the alternatives of heaven or hell which lie ahead for all. A person might profess a complete disinterest in a doctor until he realizes that he is deathly ill. Jesus said, "They that be whole need not a physician, but they that are sick" (Matthew 9:12). God's Word alone can bring the disinterested sinner to the place where he knows he is lost and wants to be saved.

3. The Deluded Person

This is the person who is in the grip of a false religion. False religions are countless in number. They ring all the changes that the inventive mind of Satan can conceive. Yet, there is one basic note common to all the false religions of the world and all the false cults of Christendom. They all teach that salvation has to be earned and that man, in some way, has to accumulate merit by means of some sacrifice or pilgrimage or penance or good work. The gospel runs counter to all this. It says, "For by grace are ye saved through faith; and that not of yourselves: it is the gift of God: not of works, lest any man should boast" (Ephesians 2:8-9). The gospel states that "the wages of sin is death; but the gift of God is eternal life through Jesus Christ our Lord" (Romans 6:23). In dealing with delusion it is helpful, of course, to be aware of the particular errors in which your contact is enslaved. It is even more helpful to know the power of God's Word to bring light to a darkened heart. It is not necessary for a captain to know where all the shoals and rocks are as he steers his vessel across the oceans of the world. All he needs to know is where the deep water is. Similarly, you may never master all the intricacies of all the world's false religious teachings. But you can know where the truth of God lies and steer your course to a person's soul along that channel.

4. The Disturbed Person

This person has been thoroughly awakened by the Holy Spirit to a deep sense of sin and need. There can be no more thrilling experience than to meet a person like this and to know that you are the right person in the right place at the right time with the right message to meet that person's need. When a seeking Savior meets a seeking sinner, salvation is always the result. The conscientious Christian will be led by the Holy Spirit to such and will taste again and again the joy which comes through leading another person into the knowledge of sins forgiven.

The Appeal

Sooner or later, in dealing with a person about his soul's salvation, the message of the gospel must be clearly presented and an invitation given to this person to accept Jesus Christ as Savior and Lord. In making this appeal there are four areas of the human personality which need to be touched—the conscience, the intellect, the emotions and the will. Cases will differ. In some cases much time will need to be spent on the conscience, in others more time will need to be spent on the intellect. Some people are, by nature, cold and calculating, others are warm and impulsive, some are tender in conscience, others easily led. Some people are reluctant to make any kind of choice. Here again we can only highlight the areas of appeal.

1. The Need to Despair

There is a sense in which every person has to *despair*. We have to come to an end of ourselves and realize that, in God's sight, we are lost and on our way to hell. In other words, to use a phrase very common in past generations, we have to come under conviction of sin. Our conscience has to be reached with the gospel.

Now a man's conscience is a very poor guide but it is an excellent goad by which the Holy Spirit prods us. He applies the Word of God to the conscience to bring a person to the place where he despairs of saving himself or of earning anything but God's wrath. His first work in the soul is to convince of the nature of sin, the need for righteousness and the nearness of judgment (John 16:8-11). Passages need to be used which speak of God's holiness (Isaiah 6:1-5; Psalm 22:2-6; Daniel 10:2-8; Revelation 1:12-17); of man's sinfulness (Job 42:1-6; Romans 1:18-3:20; Ephesians 2:1-3); of coming judgment (Matthew 13:40-42; Revelation 20:11-15; 21:8).

2. The Need to Discern

A person also needs to *discern*. He has to be taught the simplicity of God's way of salvation. Recognizing that he can do nothing to merit salvation (Ephesians 2:8-9; Romans 3:19-20; Galatians 2:16; 3:10-13; James 2:10), he must see that the Lord Jesus came into this world to be his Savior and that He died upon the cross of Calvary as his substitute and to pay the penalty of his sins (Matthew 1:21; 1 Corinthians 15:1-3; 1 Timothy 1:15; 1 Peter 2:21-24; Isaiah 53:5-6; 2 Corinthians 5:20-21). He must recognize his need for repentance—literally a change of mind which leads to a change of life (Matthew 3:8; Acts 17:30). He must see his need to personally receive Jesus Christ as his own Savior by a deliberate act (John 1:11-13; Revelation 3:20; Romans 6:23; John 3:16). He must understand that, outside of the Lord Jesus, God has no salvation to offer to men (Acts 4:12; 1 Timothy 2:5; John 14:6). He must see that apart from Christ it is impossible to live the kind of life that God demands of men (Romans 5:6; John 15:4-5).

3. The Need to Desire

A person also needs to *desire*. He must want to be in a right relationship with God. Love, joy, peace, fear, gratitude, anger—all these are powerful emotions. Any one of them might play a part in bringing a person to the place where he desires to become a Christian. Some people are saved with very little emotion involved, others weep copiously at the thought of their sins and their wrongdoings. Some are greatly elated and experience feelings of joy and liberation once they have accepted Christ. Others seem not to be greatly moved in this way. At the same time for one emotional reason or another, a person must desire to be saved. David experienced great sorrow at the thought of his sin (Psalm 51:1-17); so did the woman in the house of Simon the Pharisee (Luke 7:36-50). Fear, awe and gratitude mingled in the heart of the Philippian jailor to bring him to Christ (Acts 16:26-30). Curiosity brought Nathanael (John 1:45-51). The sheer emptiness of her life and longing for something better moved the woman at the well (John 4:6-39).

4. The Need to Decide

Finally, a person needs to *decide*. God has given to each person a will and with that will he makes the choice of whether or not he will accept Christ as his Savior. Pilate's agonizing question rings down the ages, "What shall I do then with Jesus which is called Christ?" (Matthew 27:22). To those who reject Him, Jesus said, "You will not come unto me that you might have life" (John 5:40). The Bible closes with an appeal to the will,

"Let him that is athirst come. And whosoever will, let him take of the water of life freely" (Revelation 22:17). Isaiah's prophecy closes with a solemn reminder of the consequences of not choosing aright. God says, "Yea, they have chosen their own ways, and their soul delights in their abominations. I also will choose their delusions, and will bring their fears upon them; because when I called, none did answer; when I spoke, they did not hear: but they did evil before my eyes, and chose that in which I delighted not" (Isaiah 66:3, 4).

To decide not to decide is to decide to reject Christ. The Bible warns, "How shall we escape, if we neglect so great salvation" (Hebrews 2:3). Without being obnoxious, the Christian needs to make quite clear (to those who would sidestep the issue) the seriousness of postponing a decision for Christ (Proverbs 27:1; 2 Corinthians 6:2; Proverbs 29:1).

So then, the Christian has a duty to make Christ known to the world. Amy Wilson Carmichael, a missionary to India, tells of a dream she once had. She saw a wide, sunny field where many people sat looking out over a wide expanse. Their eyes were open and they were having a picnic beneath the shade of a tree. Not far off was a gulf which yawned both deep and wide. She could see in her dream millions of people groping their way past the spot where the picnic was being held. All of them were blind. They were heading straight for the gulf and, as they came to it, they toppled over the edge with fearful cries. Here and there along the edge of the precipice stood a man, a woman, also with opened eyes, seeking to warn the oncoming crowds. But they were so few and their warnings fell, for the most part, on deaf ears. In her dream Amy Carmichael wondered why the people in the picnic did not come and help. Then she saw they were busy—making daisy chains! She awoke from her dream with a voice of thunder ringing in her ears, "What has thou done?"

Surely the parable needs no interpretation. If we have had our eyes opened, are we out there doing what really counts? Or are we making daisy chains?

> "Just one life, 'twill soon be past,
> Only what's done for Christ will last."

Remember, a young Christian, filled with the Holy Spirit and with the love of Christ, can be more effective in sharing what little he knows of Christ than perhaps a well-trained seminarian who may have a head full of theology but also may lack the reality of the living Christ in his life.

7

KNOWING GOD'S WILL

The Israelites had just been delivered from centuries of servitude in Egypt. God's will for the nation was that the people leave Egypt for ever and enter into the possession of the land of Canaan. Each step of the journey was planned by God. The Israelites were not to follow a plan drawn up by Moses. They were to follow in the way the Lord led them.

For example, the natural plan would have been to strike straight across the Sinai desert, following the coastline or the principal oases in an easterly direction, taking the shortest possible route from Egypt to the Promised Land. Instead, God led them swiftly out of Egypt and then southward, far out of the normal caravan routes, to Mount Sinai in the southern reaches of the Sinai Peninsula! The longest way around was to be the shortest way home.

And how were they led in this unexpected and unusual route? By a supernatural, fiery, cloudy column of smoke (Exodus 13:17-22). There are three important, basic lessons to be learned from this form of guidance. It was:

➤ Conspicuous Guidance

➤ Conscious Guidance

➤ Continuous Guidance

First, it was *conspicuous* guidance. Every one in the camp could see when a move was to be made or when they were to stay where they were. They could not possibly get lost in the trackless desert. The guidance of that cloudy pillar was so outstanding that the smallest child could detect the way to go.

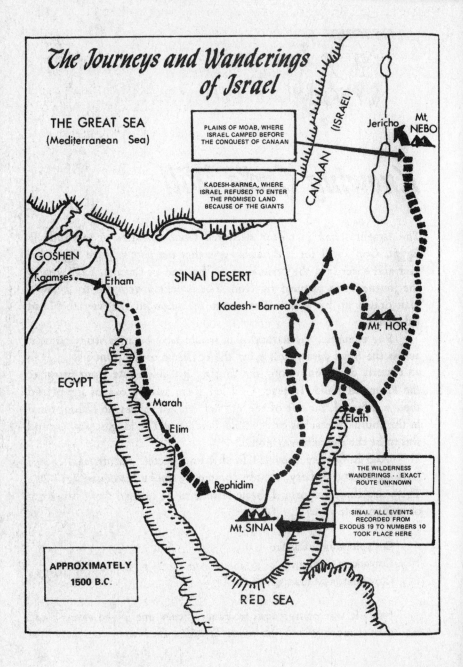

The Journeys and Wanderings of Israel

THE GREAT SEA (Mediterranean Sea)

(ISRAEL)

PLAINS OF MOAB, WHERE ISRAEL CAMPED BEFORE THE CONQUEST OF CANAAN

KADESH-BARNEA, WHERE ISRAEL REFUSED TO ENTER THE PROMISED LAND BECAUSE OF THE GIANTS

Jericho

Mt. NEBO

CANAAN

GOSHEN

Raamses

Etham

SINAI DESERT

Kadesh-Barnea

Mt. HOR

EGYPT

Marah

Elim

Elath

THE WILDERNESS WANDERINGS - - EXACT ROUTE UNKNOWN

Rephidim

Mt. SINAI

SINAI. ALL EVENTS RECORDED FROM EXODUS 19 TO NUMBERS 10 TOOK PLACE HERE

APPROXIMATELY 1500 B.C.

RED SEA

It was *conscious* guidance. There was not a person in the camp of Israel who would have the slightest shadow of a doubt about being where God wanted him to be. All doubts were banished by the cloud.

Moreover, it was *continuous* guidance. The pillar of cloud and fire continued to supernaturally lead the Israelites until at last they arrived at their ultimate destination. Now that does not mean, of course, that the path chosen was always easy. There were severe times of trial and testing along the way, but the path was safe and sure.

The question naturally arises: Does God guide Christians? He does! Moreover, there are clear principles which, if followed, will make it possible for us, today, to journey through life, conscious that we are in the known and perfect will of God. In this lesson we are going to suggest some of the principal methods of determining God's will for your life.

God's Will Must Be Desired

Obviously, if a person is to be led by God, then he must want to be led. Why should God show His will to a person who is determined to have his own way in any case? The divine principle is "The meek will he guide in judgment: and the meek will He teach His way" (Psalm 25:9). God's guidance is summed up by Solomon in the words, "Trust in the Lord with all your heart; and lean not unto your own understanding. In all your ways acknowledge him, and he shall direct your paths" (Proverbs 3:5-6). Our common sense has to be sanctified and controlled by the Spirit of God.

Many Christians who profess to want God's will for their lives really only want God to endorse their own plans, ambitions and ideas. God says, "If any man is willing to do his will, he shall know . . ." (John 7:17). There are many people also who profess to want God's will for their career but who are not the least concerned about God's will for their character. Yet for every verse in the Bible which might have some bearing on a person's career there are hundreds which reveal God's clear will concerning a person's conduct, conversation and character. Do you really desire to know God's will for your life?

God's Will May Be Discerned

Generally speaking, God's will can be discerned from three sources. He sheds light upon our path in three ways:

1. The Light of Biblical Revelation

The Psalmist could say, "Thy word is a lamp unto my feet, and a light unto my path" (Psalm 119:105). God speaks to us primarily from His Word. There are a great many things already covered in direct statement in Scripture which should settle many of the questions we might have. For example, a young woman trying to decide whether or not to marry a non-Christian need look no further for divine guidance than 2 Corinthians 6:14 where God forbids an unequal yoke. The same would be true of a businessman wondering whether or not to take an unbeliever into partnership.

Anything that is sinful, that is contrary to the Word of God and that grieves the Holy Spirit, is prohibited for a Christian. A Christian trying to make up his mind, for example, whether or not he should cheat on his income tax need look no further than Romans 13:1-9. Close fellowship with ungodly, sinful and scornful people is not God's will for a Christian (Psalm 1:1-3). On the contrary, a Christian should seek fellowship with the people of God (Hebrews 10:25).

The light of Biblical revelation is one which shines steadily. It is always there. It is our responsibility to become familiar with what God has said. Wherever the Word of God applies to our lives, its authority is absolute. It is useless to look to God for further guidance when He has already revealed His will about a given subject or situation in His Word. Hence the value and importance of a consistent daily time with God.

Some people attempt to use the Bible as a crystal ball. One popular method of attempting to find guidance is to open the Bible at random at any passage and to begin to read casually wherever the eye happens to fall. The hope is that, in some magical way, a verse or a sentence will suddenly shine light upon a proposed course of action. A well-known story illustrates the folly of such a "system." A certain man, using this "method" opened his Bible haphazardly at Matthew 27 and his eye fell on verse 5—"And he . . . departed, and went and hanged himself." Hastily he flipped the page, such a text not being to his liking! This time his eye was caught by the phrase in Luke 10:37—"Go, and do likewise." Being more alarmed than ever at "the guidance" he imagined himself to be receiving he tried again. This time he was arrested by the words in John 13:27—"What you are going to do, do quickly." It is obvious that to use the Bible in such a way is to make a mockery out of Scripture. Nobody in his right mind would read a letter or a newspaper like that. To obtain the message of the Bible it must be read thoughtfully, consistently, reverently and sensibly.

2. The Light of Spiritual Illumination

Paul tells us, "For as many as are led by the Spirit of God, they are the sons of God" (Romans 8:14). The Holy Spirit, indwelling the Christian, gently constrains him to a course of action or restrains him from a course of action. An outstanding example of this can be found in Acts 16:6-12. This intuitive, inward guidance does not come suddenly. Nor does it come without thoughtful, prayerful exercise of soul in the presence of God. *Prayer will clarify God's will.*

A word of warning is important here. The Devil can bring a deep impression to bear upon the mind or heart of a Christian. It is easy to receive a false impression. Such impressions are usually very strong and urgent at first but, upon thinking them over, they become more uncertain and sometimes absurd. On the other hand, inward impressions from the Holy Spirit are very gentle and unassuming at first but, by being put to the test, become fixed and established. False impressions invariably insist on haste with the urge, "You must do it now, or never!" Not so the gentle inward leading of the Spirit of God. God always allows plenty of time for the Christian to consider and be fully persuaded in his own mind and heart. God does not contradict His own maxim, "Wait on the Lord" (Psalm 27:14. See also David's testimony in Psalm 40:1). Impressions from God will bear patient investigation and will survive contradictions from friend and foe alike. Impressions from Satan are usually evasive and impatient at the thought of investigation. Those from God are open and free from deception. The book of James contrasts the wisdom which is from above and that which is from below. He says of the wisdom from below that it is "earthly, sensual and devilish" and tells us that the wisdom which is from above is "first pure, then peaceable, gentle, and easy to be entreated, full of mercy and good fruits, without partiality, and without hypocrisy" (James 3:15-17).

Patience will clarify God's will. Suppose you run some water from the faucet into a glass. The water is muddy and discolored. You place the glass on the table and wait. Little by little the sediment settles to the bottom of the glass and the water gradually clears. Soon it is so clear you can distinguish objects through it. It has been brought about simply by waiting.

In seeking God's will we can always afford to allow the dust and swirl of our busy lives to settle while we wait patiently for God to make His will clear. An excellent piece of advice is, "If you don't know what to do—don't do it!" Most of our mistakes come from being in too much of a hurry. But, once the issues are clear, then action must be firm and decisive.

3. The Light of Practical Confirmation

Circumstances are helpful in determining God's will but, by themselves, can be very deceptive. What looks like an open door of opportunity might lead to disaster. Lot chose Sodom because it looked like a golden opportunity for him. Abraham was content to let God overrule circumstances (Genesis 13:7-18). The sequel of the story shows how completely Lot was fooled by outward appearances. On the other hand, obstacles in the way of a desired course of action may be Satanic hindrances or they may be put there by God to test our willingness to trust Him. How, then, can we be sure?

Here again, patience is the key. The Lord said to His prophet Habakkuk, "The vision is yet for an appointed time . . . though it tarry, wait for it: because it will surely come" (Habakkuk 2:3). God usually leads us only one step at a time (Psalm 37:23-24).

While there is no single rule for guidance, we should learn to watch for the convergence of the three lights we have been discussing—the light of Biblical revelation, spiritual illumination and practical confirmation. The story is often told of Dr. F. B. Meyer who was on the bridge of a ship coming into port. He asked the captain, a friend of his, how the pilot could guide the ship into harbor with such confidence. "With this port," replied the captain, "it is really very simple. Do you see those three lights ahead? They are called 'leading lights.' At present we are at right angles to them but soon we shall make a turn and you will see those lights merge into a straight line. Then we know that we are right on course for the harbor." We too should look out for the "leading lights" to be sure that they all confirm that we are moving in the direction of God's will.

God's Will Must Be Discharged

Paul's testimony to King Agrippa, when describing how God had spoken to his soul, was this: "Whereupon, O king Agrippa, I was not disobedient unto the heavenly vision" (Acts 26:19). To know God's will and to refuse to do it is to invite disaster. It is said that on one occasion the great Duke of Wellington was approached by an officer who told him that an order he had received was impossible to execute. "Sir," said the Iron Duke, "I did not ask your opinion; I gave you my orders and they are to be obeyed."

God is too wise to make any mistakes, too loving to be unkind and too powerful to be thwarted. We can trust Him implicitly for His will is "good, perfect and acceptable" (Romans 12:2). God says, "I will instruct you and teach you in the way which you shall go: I will guide you with my eye. Be not as the horse, or as the mule, which have no understanding: whose mouth must be held in with bit and bridle, lest they come near unto you" (Psalm 32:8-9).

Think about the wise words of Abner when he sought to bring over the ten tribes to David's side. He said, "You sought for David in times past to be king over you: now then, do it!" (2 Samuel 3:17). Consider, too, the wise advice given by the Virgin Mary to those who sought her intercession. She pointed them to the Son of God and said, "Whatsoever he says unto you, do it" (John 2:5). Recall the noble words of Jonathan to David, "Whatsoever your soul desires, I will even do it for you" (1 Samuel 20:4) and the prayer of Paul that he might be permitted in God's will to go to Rome and preach the gospel there. "Making request," he said, "if by any means now at length I might have a prosperous journey by the will of God to come unto you" (Romans 1:10). The phrase "by any means" was a blank check and God filled it in at a very high figure as the book of Acts records. But Paul meant every word of it.

We write a blank check only for those we really trust. We sign the check and hand it over with the words, "*You* fill in the date, *you* fill in the amount. I can trust you implicitly." Will you give God that right in your life? Will you seek His will, determined to do it at all costs, once that will is known? Now then, do it!

8

Coping with Problems

For centuries the people had been in a condition of slavery. They were numerous, a potential threat to the nation in which they lived and a source of continuing annoyance to the government. Then the decision was made. The people would be placed in a ghetto and gradually exterminated. The plan of liquidation was simple but thorough. Every male child born to this people must be destroyed so that, within a generation, "the Jewish question" would cease to trouble Egypt.

It was at this point that God sent the people a deliver. In a sense Moses became a second founding father for Israel. Armed with Divine authority and with commensurate power, Moses began that battle of wills with Pharaoh which dominates so much of the opening chapters of the book of Exodus. One thing was sure! The Israelites must be permitted to leave Egypt clear behind. There was therefore one phrase, coming out of that conflict, which must have kindled hope in the breast of every Hebrew slave—"three days journey into the wilderness" (Exodus 3:18; 8:27). Moses was adamant on this.

The titanic struggle continued until at last, with Egypt left shattered, empty and defeated, the Israelites marched triumphantly out. Three days' journey into the wilderness! The great day dawned and the people arrived at the spot which had so fired their hopes and imaginations. There they came face to face with one of the first laws of the spiritual life— disappointment!

The place of appointment proved to be the place of disappointment. For, when Israel came to Marah (see map on page 62), three days' journey into the wilderness, "they could not drink of the waters of Marah for they were bitter" (Exodus 15:22-26). Stretched to the farthest horizons were the frightful, burning sands of the Sinai desert. The oasis at which they had arrived dashed all their hopes and great expectations to the ground. The water was acrid. Disaster stared them in the face. All the high hopes they had conceived of this place, all the mighty experiences which had accompanied their redemption, all were brought to nothing by the crushing disappointment of Marah.

The Christian and Disappointment

In his famous book, *Screwtape Letters,* C. S. Lewis gives us a flash of insight into the significance of this. You may recall that the Screwtape letters are a series of imaginary letters sent by a senior devil named Screwtape to a junior devil named Wormwood to instruct him in the art of temptation. As the letters begin, Wormwood's patient has just become a Christian. Screwtape, after warning Wormwood that he will not escape the usual penalties for his bungling of the case, sets about telling Wormwood how to make the best of this deplorable situation.

He draws Wormwood's attention to the church. He tells him to make the most of the members of the particular church Wormwood's patient has begun to attend. He tells Wormwood to work hard on the inevitable disappointment which is certain to come to the new Christian when he finds out that Christians are not perfect. He says that God "allows this disappointment to occur on the threshold of every human endeavor." Screwtape explains that God's real purpose in this is to develop spirituality, character and sonship. He warns Wormwood that while this disappointment might hold real possibilities for temptation, it is also filled with great potential for true spiritual development.

Many Christians wonder why the flush of joy and peace, which frequently accompany salvation, often subside. This is the reason. The Christian life is based on spiritual principles, not primarily on human emotional experiences. God wants us to "grow in grace and increase in the knowledge of God" (2 Peter 3:18). If we are to have our faith increased then it must be tested. Disappointments are really God's appointments, after all.

At Marah the bitter water was made sweet when Moses cast a tree into the oasis. A tree is sometimes used as a symbol in Scripture for the cross of Christ (Acts 5:30; Galatians 3:13). The spiritual lesson of Marah, then, is that we should look at our disappointments in terms of Calvary's cross. Humanly speaking, what a disappointment the crucifixion must have been to the Lord Jesus. Even His own disciples forsook Him and fled. Although He knew this would happen, the heartbreak of it all was one more burden for Him to bear. Our disappointments give us opportunities to enter into His experiences. Moreover, God never allows us to be disappointed without having some higher good in mind for us if we will but give Him the chance to make it known.

The Christian and Disaster

The Christian is not exempt from the normal calamities of life. There is a basic difference here between the Old Testament believer and the New Testament Christian. In Old Testament times, God's people, the Jews, were promised exemption from the calamities of life if they walked in obedience to His laws (Deuteronomy 28:1-14). Conversely, they were threatened with all manner of curses if they were disobedient (Deuteronomy 27:11-26; 28:15-68). Basically, the blessing of God in Old Testament times was "the blessing of the Lord, it maketh rich, and he addeth no sorrow with it" (Proverbs 10:22).

The emphasis for the Christian is quite different. The famous beatitudes of the Lord Jesus pronounce God's blessing on all kinds of conditions which we would not naturally consider happy or blessed conditions at all. "Blessed are the poor in spirit," we read. "Blessed are they that mourn . . . the meek . . . they which do hunger and thirst after righteousness . . . the merciful . . . the pure in heart . . . the peacemakers . . . they which are persecuted for righteousness sake" (Matthew 5:1-12). The reward for possessing such virtuous character, too, is not primarily material prosperity, good health, length of days and freedom from calamity but spiritual blessing. Christians have car accidents, their homes catch on fire, their children get hurt. Christians suffer loss in earthquakes, thunderstorms, tornadoes and floods. The Lord Jesus knew what it was to be hungry (Matthew 4:2), thirsty (John 4:7; 19:28), homeless (John 7:53-8:1).

The Old Testament people of God had blessings bestowed on them which were primarily temporal and earthly because essentially they were God's earthly people. Christians have blessings bestowed upon them which are primarily spiritual because they are God's heavenly people as the epistle to the Ephesians clearly emphasizes. (See also Hebrews 12:18-24.) It follows therefore that God allows things to happen to us which, if taken properly, will develop spirituality in us. That is not to say, of course, that there were no spiritual blessings for Israel in the Old Testament, because there were. Nor does it mean to say that no Christian can enjoy temporal blessings. It does mean that the emphasis is different. God has an exceedingly high destiny in mind for Christians for which He is training us both in life's advancements and in life's adversities. Paul could say "I have learned in whatsoever state I am, therewith to be content. I know both how to be abased, and I know how to abound: everywhere and in all things I am instructed both to be full and to be hungry, both to abound and to suffer need" (Philippians 4: 11-12).

The Christian and Disapproval

Not everyone is going to be delighted when someone becomes a Christian. In fact, many are going to disapprove of the decision and oppose it in every possible way. Some disapproval takes the form of violent persecution, some disapproval is more subtle. Family, social and economic pressures are often brought to bear on a Christian to force him to recant. This is especially so when the Christian is stepping out from a strong ethnic or religious background inherently opposed to evangelical Christianity. There are still countries in the world today where, to confess Christ as Savior, especially in the public form of baptism, is to invite death, or at least complete ostracization from society.

The Lord Jesus anticipated this. He said, "Think not that I am come to send peace on earth: I came not to send peace, but a sword. For I am come to set a man at variance against his father, and the daughter against her mother, and the daughter in law against her mother in law. And a man's foes shall be they of his own household" (Matthew 10:34-36). "In the world," He said, "you shall have tribulation: but be of good cheer; I have overcome the world" (John 16:33).

The history of God's people on earth has been one of persecution. The very first death in recorded history was not only a murder, it was a martyrdom. Cain slew his brother Able because Able was righteous (Genesis 4:1-16; 1 John 3:12). Opposition to Christianity began almost from the birthday of the church. The first persecution had a religious incentive behind it (Acts 4:1-21) and so did the second (Acts 5:17-42). The martyrdom of Stephen was instigated by the religious clique in Jerusalem (Acts 7) and the full scale persecutions instigated by Saul of Tarsus were inspired by religious intolerance (Acts 8:1-3; 9:1-2). Paul himself met constant opposition from religious leaders (Acts 13:44-51; 14:2-5, 19; 17:5-9, 13; 18:6; 21:27-32). Indeed the list of Paul's sufferings for Christ's sake almost passes belief (2 Corinthians 11:23-33). Persecution arose not only because the gospel challenged unscriptural religious beliefs but also because it confronted economic exploitation. On only two occasions in the book of Acts was persecution instigated by Gentiles, and on both those occasions it was because the gospel had made an unfavorable economic impact (Acts 16:16-24; 19:23-29). Peter suffered imprisonment in Jerusalem for his preaching. On this occasion the motive was political. Later on Peter suffered martyrdom for his faith (John 21:18-19; 2 Peter 1:15).

Disapproval, then, can be expected. Paul, out of his wealth of experience in suffering tells us, "Yea, and all that will live godly in Christ Jesus shall suffer persecution" (2 Timothy 3:12). A life free from opposition is the exception rather than the rule.

What should be the Christian's attitude toward disapproval? First, as Peter tells us, we should make sure that we are not being ill-treated because of things we are doing wrong. He says, "What glory is it, if, when you are buffeted for your faults, you shall take it patiently? but if, when you do well, and suffer for it, you take it patiently, this is acceptable with God" (1 Peter 2:20). He says, "Let none of you suffer as a murderer, or as a thief, or as an evildoer, or as a busybody in other men's matters. Yet if any man suffer as a Christian, let him not be ashamed; but let him glorify God on this behalf" (1 Peter 4:16). In fact, the greater part of Peter's first letter has to do with this matter of suffering and will well repay careful reading.

The last word on the subject is said by the Lord Jesus Himself. "Blessed are you when men shall revile you, and persecute you, and shall say all manner of evil against you falsely, for my sake. Rejoice, and be exceeding glad: for great is your reward in heaven: for so persecuted they the prophets which were before you" (Matthew 5:11-12).

The Christian and Disease

During His earthly ministry the Lord Jesus healed countless numbers of people of all kinds of sicknesses and disabilities. He gave sight to the blind, made the deaf to hear and the dumb to speak. He cleansed the leper, healed palsy, fever, hemorrhage, lameness and paralysis. He even raised the dead. In one chapter (Mark 5) the Lord Jesus dealt with demons, disease and death in the case of a man, a woman and a child. He healed people singly and in groups, by a touch or by a word, people close at hand and people far away.

In the history of the early church, too, miracles of healing were quite common. Peter healed a lame man, and so did Paul. Peter and Paul both raised the dead. People were healed merely by Peter's shadow falling upon them or by contact with one of Paul's handkerchiefs. Despite all this outpouring of healing power, Paul himself was a sick man and probably in constant need of a physician. (Paul's "thorn in the flesh" mentioned in 2 Corinthians 12:5-9 is thought to have been some physical disability such as epilepsy or a disfiguring eye disease. The word "infirmities" means "want of strength, weaknesses and also feebleness or sickness.") He advised Timothy to take wine as medicine and refrain from drinking water—excellent advice in a day and age which knew little or nothing of sanitation. He says, "Drink no longer water, but use a little wine for your stomach's sake and your often infirmities" (1Timothy 5:23). In a later letter to Timothy Paul mentioned the fact that he had left one of his helpers, Trophimus, "at Miletum sick" (2 Timothy 4:20).

When a Christian becomes sick it makes good common sense for him to go and see a doctor. God rarely does for us what we can do for ourselves. There are some cases where sickness is a direct result of sin (1 Corinthians 11:28-30) and in this case healing will be accomplished only when the sin is confessed and put away. It would seem that the instructions in James 5:14-15 relate to this type of sickness. Sickness can bring glory to God (John 9:1-3). But most sickness is simply part of man's lot in a sin-cursed earth, something from which Christians are no more exempt than anyone else. Sickness gives the Christian a fresh understanding of his own frailty and of his complete dependence on God for everything. Often it brings about heart searching and brings to light attitudes and traits of character a person did not realize he had. When it is permitted by God it is for a wise purpose in His will. He sometimes heals in response to prayer but He has not guaranteed to do so. It is evident that if God healed every time a sick Christian prayed for restoration of health no Christians would die of cancer, heart attacks, tuberculosis or any other illness. Many Christians have had cause to thank God for sickness which has arrested them on a wrong course and caused them to do serious thinking about life and the issues of eternity. Some of the greatest hymns of the Christian church have been written by sick people or handicapped people such as William Cowper and Fanny Crosby.

The Christian and Death

The Christian's attitude toward death is summed up in the matchless words of Paul, "For to me to live is Christ, and to die is gain" (Philippians 1:21). He said that to depart and be with Christ is "far better" (Philippians 1:23). He says, "We are confident, I say, and willing rather to be absent from the body, and to be present with the Lord" (2 Corinthians 5:8). He speaks with tremendous optimism and confidence about death. What a tremendous prospect for the Christian! It robs death of its sting. The Christian can anticipate, at death, the glorious thrill of being brought into the immediate presence of the Lord Jesus Christ. Speaking of the state in which the believer will find himself when his "earthly tabernacle" (his body) is "dissolved" (decayed by death), Paul says that we "earnestly desire" that state (2 Corinthians 5:1-2) and describes it as mortality being "swallowed up of life" (2 Corinthians 5:4).

The child of God has nothing to fear from death. Even in the Old Testament era, when not nearly so much light was given on the subject of the after life as we have now, David could speak of death as being merely "the valley of the *shadow* of death" for those who could say, "The LORD is my shepherd" (Psalm 23:1, 4). The shadow of a dog cannot bite nor can the shadow of a sword kill. The shadow of death cannot harm the child of God.

But where there is a shadow there must also be a substance and a light. The *substance* of death is separation from God. This is mentioned by David in the previous psalm (22:1). In prophetic language, he says, "My God, my God, why have you forsaken me?" These are the very words the Lord Jesus quoted when, on the cross, He (in His humanity) was separated from God when He died for us (Matthew 27:46). The substance of death is what awaits the godless when they come to the end of the journey. They go out from this life, away from the presence of all their fellows to be banished eternally from the presence of God.

As for the *light,* Jesus said, "I am the light of the world: he that followeth me shall not walk in darkness, but shall have the light of life" (John 8:12). Indeed, many Christians, having walked with the Lord all their lives, have found when they come to the portals of death that indeed "the path of the just is as the shining light that shineth more and more unto the perfect day" (Proverbs 4:18). The godless go out into the dark (Proverbs 4:19; Jude 13), the child of God goes out into the light. That does not mean, of course, that death has no fears for the Christian. It is an enemy, but as Paul says, it is the last enemy (1 Corinthians 15:26). Spurgeon used to say, "Since death is the last enemy—leave him till last!"

For the Christian "the beyond" is not only the prospect of being brought into the immediate presence of God but the prospect of resurrection too (read all of 1 Corinthians 15). And, indeed, there is the blessed hope of not having to die at all (1 Thessalonians 4:13-18) should the Lord Himself return for His own in our lifetime.

These, then, are some of the troubles which plague the Christian. They are all defeated foes. It is good to remember that we have, in God's glorious presence, One who is truly Man and who knows all about the troubles and trials of life. He is there as our Great High Priest to hear our prayers and answer them according to His own most perfect will. "Seeing then that we have a great high priest, that is passed into the heavens, Jesus the Son of God, let us hold fast our profession. For we have not an high priest which cannot be touched with the feeling of our infirmities; but was in all points tested like as we are, yet without sin. Let us therefore come boldly unto the throne of grace, that we may obtain mercy, and find grace to help in time of need" (Hebrews 4:14-16).

9

LOOKING FOR COMPANIONSHIP

The gentle slopes swept down to the blue, blue waters of the lake. Here and there amongst the hills on both sides of the lake nestled picturesque villages with quaint, old-fashioned names—Capernaum, Bethsaida, Tiberias, Chorazin. The villagers fished, farmed, herded swine. The scene was idyllic except for one thing. Up there in the cemetery, living among the dead, was a raving lunatic—a demon-possessed man. His strength was notorious, his rages horrifying to behold. More than once the villages had banded together and sent armed men to the graveyard to corner and chain the fellow only to flee from him in mortal fear when he snapped the chains like cotton thread and hurled himself upon them in demonic rage. He was the terror of all. With this man at large no one was safe.

Then Jesus came. He met this man, cast out of him the demons which held him enslaved, transformed his life and won his heart. The man, free, happy, sane and grateful wanted to go along with the Lord and the disciples. Instead, Jesus sent him home to live out his gratitude in terms of a transformed life amongst those who had known him, those who had feared him, those who had even loved him, his friends (Mark 5:1-20). For, the Christian life is to be lived in the home, in the school, at the workbench, in the ship. It is to be lived among family and friends, workmates, neighbors, rivals, enemies and even people we pass on the street. It is to be spiritual life, transforming and transfiguring every phase of social life.

In this lesson and in the next we are going to consider one set of social circumstances in which this new life is to be lived. We are going to study what the Bible says about the home, about love, courtship and marriage, about husband-wife relationships, about parent-child relationships and what it says to the single person too. How does being a Christian affect matters like these? What does the Bible say to me about being a mature person, a marriage partner, a model parent?

First then, what does the Bible have to say to the unmarried adult? It should be noted in passing that the Lord Jesus spent His adult life on earth as a single, unmarried Person. He is therefore fully able to sympathize with the special problems which face the single person. It should be noted, also, that God's standards are very high. Indeed, it is only as the life of the Lord Jesus is reproduced in us by the Holy Spirit that God's standards can be met at all. Not to meet them, however, is to invite spiritual shipwreck and inescapable damage to the life. The goal for the unmarried Christian adult is a life that is pure, a life that is patient and a life that is practical.

1. A Pure Life

God's standard is absolute. It allows for no deviation whatsoever from absolute purity when it comes to matters of inter-sexual relationships. The Bible warns against the sin of fornication (a general word for sexual impurity) by pointing to Esau (Jacob's brother) who bartered spiritual realities for a moment of fleshly lust. "Follow . . . holiness without which no man shall see the LORD . . . lest there be any fornicator, or profane person, as Esau, who for one morsel of meat sold his birthright. For you know how that afterward, when he would have inherited the blessing, he was rejected . . ." (Hebrews 12:14-17). You can read the entire story in Genesis 25 and 27. God's standards apply uniformly to single and to married people. The command "Thou shall not commit adultery" (Exodus 20:14) is amplified in the New Testament in the words, "Marriage is honorable in all, and the bed undefiled: but whoremongers and adulterers God will judge" (Hebrews 13:4).

Consider the triumph of Joseph. In two significant chapters of Genesis the Holy Spirit gives us the portrait of two brothers. Genesis 38 records the darkest blot on the page of Judah's life; the next chapter records the greatest personal triumph in Joseph's life. In both cases the testing came along the line of sex. Judah's disgrace is deliberately contrasted with Joseph's triumph. The Bible sets Joseph before us as living proof that a single person, faced with constant, fierce and overwhelming temptation to commit a sexual sin, can nevertheless win the victory if his heart is filled with proper thoughts of God. Joseph's basic reason for refusing the continued advances of his temptress was simply, "How then can I do this great wickedness, and sin against God?" (Genesis 39:9). Make sure you prayerfully read Genesis 38 and 39.

Immoral acts have their roots in impure thoughts. We must be firm in dealing with these. Paul says, "Whatever things are true, whatever things are just, whatever things are pure, whatever things are lovely, whatever things are of good report; if there be any virtue, and if there be any praise, think on these things" (Philippians 4:8). We can only consciously think of one thing at a time. When tempted to entertain impure thoughts we should deliberately think of something else. The psalmist said, "Thy word have I hid in my heart, that I might not sin against thee" (Psalm 119:11).

Consider the tragedy of David. After King David's sin—with Bathsheba—his life was never the same. The consequences of immorality are incalculable. God forgave him for his sin (2 Samuel chapters 11 and 12) but the consequences of it pursued him for the rest of his life. From then on he reaped a horrifying harvest of lust and lawlessness in his own family circle and to a large extent he lost his usefulness to God. Study the life of David as it is recorded in second Samuel with this in mind. And, when you come to the role played by Ahithophel, remember that he was Bathsheba's grandfather! The whole story is written into God's Word to warn us against sexual sin.

The popular philosophy of today is that sexual permissiveness is quite acceptable. After all, we are told, it is normal and right to indulge urges and desires planted so strongly in our very make-up. Jesus, however, said to the woman taken in adultery, "Go and sin no more," underlining the fact that we can and must control the use of our sex urges (John 8:11). That God gave these desires to us does not mean we have the right either to misuse or to ignore them. Marriage is the natural fulfillment of this drive. The Bible therefore condemns extra-marital sex but endorses and encourages sexual relations within marriage.

As for perversions and abuses of the sex drive, the Bible has nothing but the most fearful warnings for those who practice them. The cities of Sodom and Gomorrah were destroyed for giving themselves over to unnatural vices (Genesis 19). God warns that He has severe penalties for those who defile themselves in this way (Romans 1:26-27). So then, God demands a pure life. This is His standard for all men and it is most certainly His standard for a Christian.

2. A Patient Life

One of the hardest things for a single person to do is to wait for God to bring the right partner along. In our culture, dating begins in the teens and the philosophy is to keep playing the field until the right one is found. God's plan is better although, admittedly, we all find it is harder and it calls for greater restraint. Few ever try it but those who do never cease to thank God for the marvel and wonder of His choice. Start to pray about life's partner before you stumble upon someone you yourself might choose. In this way you will find God's will easier to determine and to accept.

The Divine *ideal* for marriage is given to us in the story of the very first marriage. You will find the record in Genesis 2:18-25. To begin with, Adam dwelt alone in a perfect environment in the garden of Eden. He was happy, busy and content. Then God brought the animal creation to Adam for naming. Adam would undoubtedly observe that each animal had its appropriate mate. In this way God awakened in Adam a sense of lack, a realization that he, himself, was without a partner. This awareness was awakened in Adam by God and was not artificially aroused by Adam's own impatient behavior. God never awakens a legitimate longing He does not intend to fill. If we awaken desires by our own foolishness that is another matter.

Next, God put Adam to sleep and took from his side that from which He created Eve. In other words, there is a sense in which Adam went to sleep in the will of God, leaving the whole matter of finding a partner to God. This is where we so easily fail. We take matters into our own hands and become increasingly desperate, insecure and unhappy when things fail to materialize as we plan. Often, too, our choice, in the end, is a sad second best. (True, God often overrules our mistakes and turns them into blessings but that is not the point here.) Finally, God brought to Adam the woman He had created especially for him and Adam awoke from his sleep to look into the face of the one and only woman in the world.

That is the Divine ideal. You can trace the same principle in the romance of Isaac and Rebekah (Genesis 24) and elsewhere in the Old Testament. Our problem is we cannot wait for God. We do not really believe that God's will is as good, as perfect and as acceptable as He says it is (Romans 12:2). We think our will is better and that we know best. We need to learn the secret of a patient life. The Christian who is not patient before marriage will certainly have to learn patience afterwards, especially if he makes a serious mistake in his choice. For divorce is not in God's plan for a child of God (Matthew 5:31, 32; 19:3-11).

Often an impatient Christian, looking for a life partner, will contemplate marrying an unbeliever. Such a step is surely out of the will of God. The

Bible speaks plainly on this. It says, "Be not unequally yoked together with unbelievers: for what fellowship has righteousness with unrighteousness? and what communion has light with darkness? and what concord has Christ with Belial? or what part has he that believes with an infidel? and what agreement has the temple of God with idols? for you are the temple of the living God . . ." (2 Corinthians 6:14-16). This is a sound principle. Marriage links two lives together in the closest of intimacy. If there is no spiritual affinity then disaster often follows. Even the most ideal marriages have their stresses and strains without building in a basic and inevitable weakness right from the start.

3. A Practical Life

Until such a time as God clearly indicates the partner He has chosen, it would be best for the single person to concentrate on serving the Lord with all his might. Paul, who apparently was single himself, could see advantages in being unmarried. While being the first to admit that not all people have the gift for celibacy, Paul could still write, "I say therefore to the unmarried and widows, It is good for them if they abide even as I" (1 Corinthians 7:6-9).

It is natural for most people to want to be married. However, the single person does have some great advantages when it comes to serving the Lord—advantages in terms of time, money and freedom. These advantages can be lavished on the Lord and His work. Paul says, "He that is unmarried cares for the things that belong to the Lord, how he may please the Lord; but he that is married cares for the things of the world, how he may please his wife" (1 Corinthians 7:32, 33). Obviously he is not depreciating marriage but is emphasizing the advantages that accrue to the single person. And, of course, he is assuming the unmarried person is a dedicated Christian. A carnal Christian is going to be discontent no matter what his circumstances.

Surely the Lord who made us, who knows our personalities and make-up better than we do, can be trusted to do what is best for us. He says, "The Lord will give grace and glory: no good thing will He withhold from them that walk uprightly" (Psalm 84:11). Since He has also said, "It is not good that the man should be alone" (Genesis 2:18), it follows that if the Lord withholds a marriage partner it must be because He has some higher good in mind.

In the meantime there are many compensations for the dedicated Christian and many openings for service which, if pursued, will fill the life to the full and more than compensate for any imagined loss. Single people who long for the love of children can find this love in working with children in camps, hospitals and schools. Single people can bring the fragrance of a Christ-centered life to gladden the lives of the lonely, the aged, the infirm, the outcast. Mission fields all over the world are looking for men and women. The Macedonian call, "come over . . . and help us" (Acts 16:9) is still ringing out from a lost world. Single people are far more mobile and able to respond to the challenge than married people with families. (Incidentally, almost all the missionary activity recorded in the book of Acts was carried on by single people.) It is a positive sin to sit and mope because God has not seen fit to bless with a marriage partner. Perhaps the very one He has chosen is waiting in another country on some far-off mission field, or even a few blocks down the street in a place of service He has in mind.

If you are single, bring your life to the Lord right now. Say to him, "Here I am, Lord. Until you see fit to alter it, I am determined to be content with my present state. Help me, by Your Spirit, to live a life that is pure, that is patient, that is practical, a life in the centre of that good and acceptable and perfect will of Yours." There is no real substitute for God's will in your life.

10

BUILDING THE HOME

Old-fashioned romantic novels always ended with the rugged hero marrying the starry eyed heroine and with a pat phrase telling us that they "lived happily ever after." Well, maybe they did. But certainly not without some far-reaching and inevitable adjustments. Being a Christian does not eliminate the need for adjustments in marriage but it certainly should make the process smoother.

In our last lesson we studied what the Bible says to the single person. In this lesson we are going to see what it has to say about Christian marriage. Read Ephesians 5:22-6:4 and also 1 Corinthians 7.

The Marriage Partner

When we purchase an expensive and intricate piece of equipment, we are always careful to read the manufacturer's instructions to make sure we do not break something. It is evident that the manufacturer knows what is best for the smoothest operation of his product. When the instructions say, "Press button 'A' before you push lever 'B' " it is because this is the right order to follow if the equipment is to work. To reverse this order will not improve the performance of the machine and might do it lasting damage, especially if non-compliance with the instructions is continual.

Marriage is a far more complex mechanism than a piece of manufactured equipment. In marriage two people with different personalities, backgrounds, temperaments, outlooks and often different educational, social, religious and racial environments are welded together in a most lasting and complex relationship. Marriage was God's invention for the human race, and He intends it should function smoothly. He has given us instructions in His Word, therefore, for ensuring harmony in the home. It is foolish to ignore these instructions. It is little wonder many marriages do not work when God's order is ignored and His principles neglected. Let's examine these principles.

1. The Wife's Role—Submissive Love for Her Husband

The first essential in Ephesians 5 is addressed to the wife. She is told by God to submit willingly to her husband. It is easy to see why this might offend the liberated woman of today, so let's take time to consider *the principle* which underlies this requirement.

Men, *as men*, and women, *as women*, are equal before God. This is clearly taught in Galatians 3:28. It is in the marriage relationship that the husband is said, in Ephesians 5, to be the head. God says, "The husband is the head of the wife even as Christ is the head of the church." This is a most helpful and instructive analogy. In 1 Corinthians 11:3-16 the whole concept of headship is further developed, especially as that principle relates to the fellowship of a local church.

We (the church) are viewed as the bride of Christ. So greatly did He (God's Son, the Lord of Glory) set His love upon us (this church of His) that to win us He laid aside His glory. He took humanity upon Himself, entered fully into human life, went to Calvary and died to make us His own. But how unlovely we were in our sin and shame! He cleansed us, clothed us and lifted us higher than the angels. He made us His church, His bride, and destined us to share His throne, His glory and His power. And He loves us with a love beyond compare. The church responds to Him with loyalty and love. She yields to Him in all things. He is her Lord, her Redeemer, her Groom. Her greatest joy is to please Him.

This is the analogy Paul draws. "The husband is the head of the wife as Christ is the head of the church." The principle is the same in both realms— *surpassing love* on the one hand; *submissive loyalty* on the other.

There is *a privilege* in such submission as well as a principle. Paul says, "As the church is subject unto Christ, so let the wives be to their own husbands in everything." There is a direct relationship between the two. When a wife gives submissive love to her husband she is showing far more than the beauty of divine order in her home, good though that is in itself. She is displaying to all the universe a picture of the eternal relationship which exists between Christ and His church. In other words, by her submission, she is participating in an order which has cosmic significance.

The apostle Peter illustrates the principle by reminding us that Sarah called Abraham "Lord" (1 Peter 3:1-6). Trace the story of Abraham and Sarah (Genesis 11-23) and you will find that Sarah's submission to Abraham was in the face of several very serious lapses of loyalty on Abraham's part. The Bible honors her for her submission despite Abraham's failures and faults.

In contrast with Sarah, the Bible records the conniving of Rebekah against her husband Isaac (Genesis 27). Isaac's home was a place of discord and domestic strife and is in sharp contrast with Abraham's (Genesis 18:19). Study Isaac's home life. You will see that Isaac was an unspiritual father, Rebekah was an unsurrendered wife, Esau was an unsaved son and Jacob was an unscrupulous brother. The wrangling which went on in that home stemmed to a large extent from Rebekah's unyieldedness.

2. The Husband's Role—Sacrificial Love for the Wife

a. *The Priorities of Marriage.* The second essential is addressed to the husband. He is to love his wife with a Christlike devotion and sacrifice. In Ephesians 5, Paul shows that a husband's love for his wife is to be in *the example of the Savior's love.* He says, "Husband's, love your wives, even as Christ also loved the church, and gave himself for it." Could love be greater than that? It should not be difficult for a wife to love a husband who is prepared to go to any sacrifice for her well-being. The Lord Jesus, in His love for the church, looks beyond all her blemishes and imperfections, such as denominational divisions, to that day when she will be perfect. He sees in her a beauty which is eternal, glorious to behold. He loves His church with a love that knows neither measure nor end. The Holy Spirit sets up that love as the standard and the norm of the love a husband is to show to his wife.

The husband's love is not only to be in the example of the Savior's love, it is also to be *an extension of his self love.* Paul says, "So ought men to love their wives as their own bodies. He that loves his wife loves himself. For no man ever yet hated his own flesh; but nourishes and cherishes it, even as the Lord the church." Well put, Paul! We love our own bodies even if they are sickly, old and decrepit. We nurse them and nourish them. We dress them up in the best finery we can afford. We feed them three square meals a day, exercise them, indulge them, pamper them or toughen them as our nature dictates. We rush them off to the doctor when they are sick. We hang on to them as long as we possibly can, doing our utmost to keep them out of the clutches of the grave. All the care and consideration a man gives to his body he is to give to his wife.

The secret of Sarah's loyalty to Abraham lay in Abraham's love for Sarah. We have only to look at his grief when Sarah died to realize how deep and real was his love for her (Genesis 23:2). It is an interesting thought, by the way, that Sarah's name meant "princess." Every time Abraham spoke to Sarah he called her princess. It would not be hard for most women to call a husband "lord" who habitually called her "princess."

b. *The Permanence of Marriage.* Marriage is intended to be a permanent institution. Paul concludes his great thesis on marriage with the words, "For this cause shall a man leave his father and mother, and shall be joined unto his wife, and they two shall be one flesh. This is a great mystery: but I speak concerning Christ and the church." This is quoted from Genesis 2:24. The Lord Jesus is quoting from the same primeval law of marriage added "What therefore God hath joined together, let not man put asunder" (Matthew 19:5, 6).

The only condition under which the New Testament permits a divorce is on the ground of sexual unfaithfulness (Matthew 5:31, 32). The Lord's high standard on marriage astonished even His disciples (Matthew 19:10) but He did not lower it on that account. The Lord went to the root of the matter on divorce by declaring that "hardness of heart" was at the bottom of it (Mathew 19:8). Such hardness was tolerated by the Old Testament principle of *law* but it is not allowed by the New Testament principle of *love.*

Where one of the marriage partners is not a Christian, special problems arise. These are discussed in 1 Corinthians 7. The believing partner is expected to so live Christ that eventually the unsaved partner will surrender to the claims of Christ too. Moreover the godly testimony of the Christian partner is to have a sanctifying influence on the children. But, if the unbelieving partner decides to walk out of the marriage, that is his responsibility. The saved partner is to let him go but is not to aggravate the domestic situation in order to provoke such a separation; the way must always be left open for reconciliation. These are high and holy standards. It is little wonder that Paul prefaces his teaching on Christian marriage, in Ephesians, by first giving instructions about being filled with the Spirit. It is only a Spirit-filled Christian who can meet the divine ideal.

The Model Parent

Children are a great blessing in the home and a solemn responsibility. They are called "an heritage of the Lord" (Psalm 127:3). God says the man who has many children is a happy man (Psalm 127:5). In his teaching on the relationships between parents and children Paul is balanced and moderate. He gives both sides of a very important question.

1. Children Must Face the Principle of Obedience

Notice, first, *the requirement*. Paul says to children, "Obey your parents in the Lord: for this is right. Honor your father and your mother." The entire will of God for a child is summed up in that statement. We are living in an age when disobedience to parents is maturing into a brawling defiance of all authority (2 Timothy 3:2—read this in its context). The root cause of the unrest in society is in the total lack of discipline and obedience in the home. A child who has never learned to obey his father and mother is going to have no respect for authority anywhere, whether it is vested in his teachers at school, in the person of his employer at work, in the policemen on the street corner or in the magistrate on the bench. To *obey* has to do with the child's duty; to *honor* has to do with his disposition. God wants a child to render cheerful, warm and willing obedience to parents.

The reason for this rule of obedience is given next. Paul says "for this is right"; in other words it is the correct thing for a child to do. He says that the commandment to children to obey their parents is "the first commandment with promise." In other words, it is the commanded thing to do. Paul, of course, is quoting from the fifth of the Ten Commandments (Exodus 20:1-17). It is significant that the Lord Jesus, as a boy of twelve, went back to Nazareth with His mother and with Joseph and was subject unto them (Luke 2:51). So long as He was a minor He submitted Himself to the authority of His mother and His foster father. There is no higher example in the Bible for a child to follow than this.

The reward for obedience is stated both in the Old Testament and in the New Testament. Quoting further from the Ten Commandments, Paul says to children, "That it may be well with you, and you may live long on the earth." In other words longevity of life depends, to a certain extent, on learning obedience to parents. In the home a child learns the great principle of obedience which stands him in good stead when he gets out into the world. The character which is formed in the home determines the kind of person the child will become. It goes a long way toward determining whether the child will have a smooth path through life to an honored and venerable old age.

2. Parents Must Face the Possibility of Oppressing

Parents need to exercise godly care in disciplining their children. It is easy to be too indulgent, but it is just as easy to be too harsh. Both extremes are wrong.

Parents need to learn *the correct amount of discipline* which should be administered. Paul says, "Fathers, provoke not your children to wrath." One translation renders this, "Fathers, don't over-correct your children." It is easily done and really amounts to oppression and bullying. God is not one-sided in His commands. Children are to honor and obey their parents but parents, especially fathers, are not to bully and nag their children. Some parents are totally unreasonable in their demands and brutal in their discipline. The Bible endorses the wholesomeness of corporal punishment (Proverbs 13:24; 19:18; 22:15; 23:13; 29:15) but it does not give license to a parent to unmercifully flog his child. It is all too easy to make demands or extort punishments in anger. Such behavior is not Christian. Firmness and fairness are the royal rules for parents.

Parents need to learn *the correct approach to discipline.* Paul says, "Don't make it difficult for them to obey the commandment." This can be done when parents expect children to fulfill tasks which are beyond their strength and when parents set unreasonable goals and time limits. It can be done, psychologically, by choosing the wrong moment or the wrong motive in laying down the law. It can be done by creating an atmosphere of fear, hostility, mistrust or suspicion. It can be done by failure to follow through on warnings, thus conditioning the child to believe that the parent does not really mean what he says.

Parents need to learn *the correct aim in discipline.* Paul says, "Bring them up in the nurture and admonition of the Lord." In other words, children need to be taught what to believe (the "nurture" of the Lord) and how to behave (the "admonition" of the Lord). Happy is the home where these divine principles are followed.

The time to begin with children is when they are very young. It is surprising at what a tender age an infant will assert his own will in defiance of the will of the parent. It happens in the cradle itself. A parent who does not break a child's rebellious will, at a tender age, need not be surprised if that child grows up to break his parent's heart.

Some years ago a woman wrote to a columnist complaining that her seventeen year old son was rebellious, keeping company with the wrong crowd, becoming involved with the law and refusing to listen to anything she said. The columnist's reply was terse and to the point. "Shrink him down to seventeen months," he said, "and begin all over again." Those who follow the Bible blueprint need never come to that.

Parents need to learn *the correct attitude for discipline*. A real effort needs to be made to keep the channels of communication open within the family. Parents should talk to their children in a sympathetic and understanding way about the children's interests, problems, hopes, frustrations and fears. When children express doubts about spiritual matters, parents ought not to panic. Often the children are groping for a real faith of their own to replace the second-hand faith they have perhaps inherited.

Parents should make time to read the Bible and pray with their children. They should invite the children to participate, to question, to discuss the Scripture passage being read. Parents and children ought to pray together. It is a good idea for parents to tell the Lord their own faults and failings at times during family devotions. This lets children know that their parents realize that they are not perfect themselves. It is a good idea for parents to think back to when they were children themselves and to recall the things they said and did. It will help parents to refrain from imposing unfair, artificial and unreasonable standards of behavior on their children.

Many parents have found that a good time to empathize with their children about spiritual things is after the children are in bed in that magic "no-man's-land" of time between climbing into bed and falling asleep.

11

EXPLORING THE BIBLE

There is no book in all the world like the Bible. It comes to us from God (see chapter 2) and deals with matters of the most momentous import. A little girl once wanted to give her author father a birthday gift and decided to give him a Bible. Having purchased the gift, she wanted to write something appropriate on the flyleaf. To generate some ideas she consulted books on her father's library shelves many of which had been sent to him by other authors. At last she decided what to write, carefully inscribed the message, wrapped the gift and waited with eager anticipation for the moment when her father would open it. The day came and the present was unwrapped and admired. "See what I've written, Daddy," said the little girl. The father turned to the flyleaf and there he read: "To my dear dad—with the compliments of the author!" It was a notable mistake! For that is exactly the way the Bible comes to us. It comes to us directly from the mind of God.

Exploring the Bible is an adventure in living. *Personally,* it will expand your mind by occupying your thoughts with the greatest concepts ever conveyed to men. *Domestically,* it will build dynamic, vital, workable, and rewarding family relationships. *Socially*, it will make you a wholesome, constructive, helpful and involved member of your community, able to relate with insight, integrity and decisiveness to local, national and world affairs. *Spiritually*, it will make you a useful, functioning, vibrant member of your local church.

While we may realize that the Bible well repays careful study, where do we begin? The Bible is such a vast book and, in some ways, a very complex book. At the same time it is a book which will yield its treasures to any devout Christian willing to patiently and consistently spend time seeking to grasp it and understand it and prepared to obey its teachings as they are unfolded to him. In this lesson we are going to consider the task and the tools of Bible study.

The Task

Bible study is work. It is true that the Bible can be read and enjoyed as literature for the leisure hour. Its weighty truths, however, can only be made ours by diligent and patient work. This was why Paul said to young Timothy, "Study (literally, give diligence) to show yourself approved unto God, a workman that needs not to be ashamed, rightly dividing the word of truth" (2 Timothy 2:15).

1. The Possible Realms of Bible Study

The first, and in many ways the most important, method of Bible study is *the survey method*. It is the method we use when we study a map. First with a sweeping glance we take in the continents, moving rapidly to the one in which our interest lies. We briefly note the countries and pass on to the one we wish to study, observing particularly which nations border on it. We then look at the regions into which that particular country is divided, concentrate on the region we want and then notice carefully where the cities are located within that region. By the time we find the city that interests us, we have a fair idea of where it is in relation to the nation as a whole, to the continent in general and to the world at large. The survey approach gives us a proper perspective by relating the part to the whole.

The Empire State Building is the obvious place to start when visiting New York. From this vantage point the visitor can see how the city is laid out and the relationship of one suburb to another. Similarly, to avoid unnecessary confusion, if you are studying the Bible for the first time, you should do a brief survey of the whole. This will ensure that you have some idea of the order in which events occur, some grasp of the time periods involved; a concept of geography and history, manners and customs; an understanding of the varying ways in which God dealt with different people at given times; an idea of the way truth was progressively revealed over the long span of Bible history and a comprehension of how, why and when the various books came to be written and what they contain.

A Bible survey does much to help us avoid confusion on these matters. How important it is, for example, to realize that Isaiah and Jeremiah (whose books come next to each other in the Bible) actually lived about a century apart and that they lived in worlds as different from one another as our world is from that of our grandfathers. How helpful it is, too, when studying Paul's letters to the Corinthians, to know at what stage in Paul's missionary career the church at Corinth was founded and what particular set of circumstances prompted the writing of those two letters.

For a Bible survey there is no substitute for the continual reading of the Bible (a whole book at a time) and for wide reading of authors who explain Bible backgrounds. Survey courses are particularly helpful to begin with as they chart a course and set a pace for an initial overall view of the Bible. We suggest *Summary of the Bible* (a very brief survey course). Write or call ECS Ministries for more information. This course may be available at the school from which you obtained this course.

The *analytical method* of Bible study is the opposite of the survey method. For example, after surveying a painting of a landscape, a person might then take his magnifying glass and begin to count the petals on a flower away off in a remote corner of the picture. The analytical approach takes a book of the Bible, a section, a chapter, or even a single verse and breaks it down into its component parts. First you discover and caption the major themes of the portion. These you then divide and sub-divide until the entire portion is broken up into well labeled parts.

Let us apply this process to Psalm 32. You will notice, at the outset, that this is a psalm of David, it is all about sin, and that it applies to the incident in David's life recorded in 2 Samuel 11-12. This historical setting should be studied because it casts much light on the psalm. First read the psalm several times looking for the overall theme and ways in which this theme is handled. You will observe that the psalm is in two parts. Verses 1-7 show how David viewed his sin and verses 8-11 show how God views sin. These major divisions might be captioned—I. How The Sinner Views His Sin (1-7) and II. How The Savior Views Our Sin (8-11).

Examine each of these sections more closely. Read verses 1-2 and note the expression: "Blessed is the man whose sin is forgiven" and similar expressions. In these verses David tells us that his sin was **cleansed**. Now read verses 3-4 and see what happened to David when he pretended he had not sinned, when his sin was **concealed**. In verse 5 David tells how he acknowledged his sin; his sin was **confessed**. In verses 6-7 he finds there is a refuge from sin in God and he anticipates deliverance when tempted again. In other words, his sin was **conquered**.

Look now at the second segment of the psalm and note that there are four themes, one for each of the four remaining verses, giving God's view of human sin. In verse 8 God offers to lead David into right ways. In other words, we need to be **guided**. In verse 9 He brings before David the need of willing submission to God's will. We need to be **governed**. In verse 10 God promises to protect those who trust Him from the evil consequences which follow wrong doing. We need to be **guarded**. Last of all, in verse 11, God challenges David to rejoice. We need to be **gladdened**.

The full analysis of the psalm can be set out thus:

I. HOW THE SINNER SEES HIS SIN (1-7)

    A. Sin Cleansed (1-2)

    B. Sin Concealed (3-4)

    C. Sin Confessed (5)

    D. Sin Conquered (6-7)

II. HOW THE SAVIOR SEES OUR SIN (8-11)

    We need to be:

    A. Guided (8)

    B. Governed (9)

    C. Guarded (10)

    D. Gladdened (11)

Other methods of Bible study include the *topical method*, the *doctrinal method* and the *biographical method*. The method of going about these types of study is similar in each case. The topical method is to take a frequently mentioned topic found in the Bible and see what the Bible, as a whole, has to say about it. (This may be done with the help of the tools mentioned later on in this lesson.) For example, you might want to systematize what the Bible says about death, about worship, about prayer, about faith, about giving or about any one of the hundreds of topics mentioned in Scripture. Similarly, you might want to do the same with the great doctrines of the Bible. What does the Bible say about God, about man, about angels, about sin, about salvation, about heaven? In the same way you might wish to study the characters of people mentioned in the Bible, many of whom are fascinating and whose lives are full of instruction.

In each case you would seek out the chief places in the Bible where the topic, the doctrine or the character is mentioned and collect all the data you can from those passages. (The Bible is not like a garden, where everything is found in orderly rows; it is like a forest.) From the mass of information collected you would need to produce some kind of order and to do this you would simply follow the steps outlined for the analytical method. You would group the material into major themes and sub-themes, giving each an appropriate caption. In this way you systematize the miscellaneous collection of facts previously assembled.

There are other methods of Bible study. Those suggested here will get you off to a good start and do not require technical knowledge and familiarity with the original languages of the Bible as would, for example, the grammatical method. The more you learn of the Bible, the more your study will become profitable. Knowledge learned in one place will cast light upon research being done in another.

2. The Principal Rules of Bible Study

Bible study has its rules. False teaching usually arises from a failure to follow sound principles of interpretation (i.e., hermeneutics). There are a considerable number of these rules but for the purpose of this lesson we are going to discuss briefly only some of the major ones.

First and foremost is the *literal rule,* often called "the golden rule" of Bible study. This rule states that, as far as possible, the Bible must be taken literally. God means what He says and says what He means. If the plain sense makes common sense we should seek no other sense. In other words, when we are studying a passage of Scripture, we should not be trying to read into the text all sorts of fanciful, imagined meanings. We should read the Bible as we would read any other book. When we read Shakespeare, for example, we immediately relate the text to the unfolding plot of the play. We do not try to read into the text some hidden meaning, for Shakespeare's plays are not mysterious allegories under guise of which he attacked the Establishment of his day; they are entertaining stories intended to be enjoyed as they are preformed on the stage. True, an understanding of the Elizabethan age will help us to better appreciate Shakespeare but it would be folly to try to read into Shakespeare fanciful allegorical meanings the playwright never intended his plays to sustain. Similarly, an understanding of the grammar, the history and the culture behind the Bible text is vital and important if the Bible is to be properly understood. But we must not read our own ideas and theories into the Bible. We must let the Bible convey literal truth in a normal way.

The next rule is closely connected with the first one. We can call it the *poetical rule* for, while it is true the Bible must be understood literally, the form in which that literal truth is conveyed is often poetic. The Bible is full of imagery, symbolism and figures of speech; these forms of expression are not to conceal God's mind but rather to emphasize truth and to give it color. We use figures of speech constantly in ordinary conversation. When an American, for example, speaks of "Uncle Sam" everyone knows he is referring pictorially to the nation just as an Englishman would refer to his nation under the symbol of John Bull. If a person says that he "completely lost his head" we know what he means. He does not mean that his head fell off his body and he was unable to find it; he simply means he lost control of himself. The figure of speech, however, lends drama and vividness to the thought the speaker had in mind.

There are some two hundred figures of speech in the Bible. There is, for example, metaphor—"all flesh is grass" (Isaiah 40:6); simile—"all we like sheep have gone astray" (Isaiah 53:6); personification—"the earth opened her mouth" (Numbers 16:32) and hyperbole—"the world itself could not contain the books that should be written." These are just a few examples of the way in which the Bible uses poetic forms of expression to convey literal truth. When reading the Scripture we do not look for exotic, mystical and far-fetched meanings behind the use of poetic imagery and symbolism. We look for the literal truth normally conveyed by the use of such language.

The *spiritual rule* is important for not everyone can understand God's truth. Paul says that "the natural man receiveth not the things of the spirit of God: for they are foolishness unto him: neither can he know them because they are spiritually discerned" (1 Corinthians 2:14). Before a person can really understand the Bible he needs to be born again and guided by the Holy Spirit. He must approach the Bible with a humble, teachable spirit willing to accept the authority of God's Word and to obey it when the truth has a bearing on his moral or spiritual conduct. God will not give more light upon the Scripture unless we are responding to the light we have. To study the Bible merely as an academic exercise is to invite eventual disaster, for God holds us accountable to live up to the light that we have.

The *contextual rule* is very important. It has been well said that "a text without a context is a pretext." In other words it is possible to make a verse of Scripture support a completely unscriptural theory simply by taking it out of its context. Many false cults are guilty of doing this. They bolster wrong teachings with isolated verses pulled from various parts of the Bible and not only misapply them but frequently make the verses say things they were never intended to say. For instance the Bible uniformly teaches that salvation is by faith and not by works. Those who disagree with this frequently support their error by quoting Philippians 2:12 which says, "work out your own salvation with fear and trembling." Usually the quotation is cut off right at that point. The very next statement in the following verse puts the text into context for it says, "For it is God who works in you both to will and to do of his good pleasure." The context guards against the error. Isolated texts can only be used to support a doctrine when they are used in a way which does not violate the context from which they are taken.

Numerous other rules could be listed but these will be sufficient to get you off to a good start in your Bible study. The diligent student will want to start practicing the principles outlined here. In addition, he may wish to purchase books on hermeneutics to learn other rules of Bible study.

The Tools

The tools available for Bible study vary greatly from country to country and from language to language. In the English language, for instance, there are thousands of good, helpful books available covering all phases of Bible study. In Ethiopia the number of available commentaries could be held in two hands. Here we will mention just a few of the more basic and essential books which every serious Bible student would be well advised to add to his library.

First, make sure you have *a good Bible* with clear, readable type and, preferably, one with cross references in the margin.

Next, every student needs a *concordance*. A concordance is a specialized type of dictionary which lists every word in the Bible and gives all the references where that word is to be found. It is an invaluable aid for locating texts. For example you might want to find the verse quoted above, "work out your own salvation with fear and trembling." Provided you can recall one of the words in the text you can find the reference in your concordance. You can look it up under "work," "own," "salvation," "your," "fear" or "trembling." The less frequently the word is used in the Bible, the easier it will be for you to find it; but under any of these words you will find enough of the verse printed out to enable you to recognize it. Alongside the verse you will find the reference—Philippians 2:12. The beginner need not invest in a high priced concordance usually used by more advanced students for checking on original Greek and Hebrew words. A simple, straight-forward concordance is adequate for most needs.

A Bible dictionary is a very useful book to have. It gives all kinds of information on almost every possible Bible topic. It is packed with archaeological, geographical, historical, cultural, biographical, textual, analytical and chronological facts. A good Bible dictionary is a mine of information. The student can save himself from very serious blunders by consulting one. For example, the Joshua mentioned in Deuteronomy 34:9 is not the same person as the Joshua mentioned in Zechariah 3:1. To confuse the two might be a harmless blunder but it hardly makes for accuracy in Bible study. A Bible dictionary will quickly enable you to see what's what and who's who.

Commentaries are many and varied and need to be bought with a great deal of care. A commentary is only as good as its author. If the author holds unsound views, those are bound to come out in the commentary. The test to be applied to any book purchased as an aid to Bible study is the test applied by the Bereans to the teaching of Paul. Luke says, "These [the Bereans] were more noble than those in Thessalonica, in that they received the word with all readiness of mind, and searched the Scriptures daily, whether those things were so" (Acts 17:11). Rather than buy an unsound commentary, check first with a mature and well taught Christian and get his opinion on it. Your instructor will be glad to advise you on *some* good basic books to purchase. The serious Bible student will want to be adding new books to his library continually—and reading them too.

One of the most helpful ways for a Christian to increase his grasp of the Bible is to study good *correspondence courses.* No doubt you have found this out already! The advantage of a correspondence course is that you are put in touch with an instructor who will help you, answer your questions, correct your mistakes, guide you and take a personal interest in your progress. Also whole series of such guided studies can be undertaken which will lead you on in a methodical way toward Christian maturity. You should seriously consider pursuing your studies in this way. The advantages of studying the Bible by correspondence far outweigh the costs involved which, in any case, are often modest and frequently surprisingly low.

As in choosing your books, choose your correspondence school with care. The instruction you receive will only be as good as the Institution which offers the courses and the teaching. Some false cults lure the unwary into all kinds of spiritual heresy by offering free courses. If you are in doubt about a school be sure to ask a mature Christian for advice. Your instructor will be glad to help. In fact, perhaps your best next move would be to write to the school from which you acquired this course and ask what other courses they have to offer and what they would suggest you study next.

12

ENJOYING THE FELLOWSHIP

When people think of the church, they usually call to mind that great, organized system of religion which began to develop about the second or third century of the Christian era, which became the official religion of the Roman Empire under Constantine and which today is represented by the Greek, Roman and Established State churches and by the various Protestant churches organized on denominational or independent lines. But is this really the church, or is this better described as Christendom? What is the church? What does the New Testament say about it? These are the questions we shall seek to answer in this lesson.

The Mystery of the Church

The church as such is not a subject of direct Old Testament revelation. Its coming, its character and its continuation are fully revealed only in the New Testament. It is actually called "a mystery" by Paul (Ephesians 3:9-10; 5:32). A "mystery," in the New Testament, is not something mysterious. It is something previously hidden from men, something which could not be discovered by human reasoning and logic, but something which has now been revealed to men by God. There are a number of such "mysteries" revealed in the New Testament and the church is one of them.

Three very important illustrations are given to us in the New Testament to help us comprehend what God had in mind when He brought the church into being on the Day of Pentecost (fifty days after the Lord's resurrection and ten days after His ascension into heaven).

1. The Church as a Body

The church is likened to a body of which Christ is the head (1 Corinthians 12:12-27; Romans 12:4-5). Each member of a body is important, each shares the same spirit and the same life, each has its own particular function to perform, each feels for the other, each takes its orders directly from the head. The true Head of the church is Christ Himself. Here, the test as to whether or not a person belongs to the church is this—is he related to Christ in a real, vital, intimate way so that he shares the life of Christ and the Spirit of Christ, enjoys fellowship with other true Christians, and lives in obedience to Christ?

2. The Church as a Bride

The church is likened to a bride for whom Christ is the Groom (Ephesians 5:22-32; 2 Corinthians 11:2). Here the test as to whether or not a person is a member of the church is this—is he looking for the return of Christ (see chapter 2), longing for Him and living for Him in the way a bride does an absent bridegroom? Is there a definite love relationship between that person and the Lord Jesus?

3. The Church as a Building

The church is likened to a building of which Christ is the foundation (Ephesians 2:19-22; 1 Corinthians 3:11; 10:4). The Lord told Peter that he would play an important part in helping to found the church (Matthew 16:17-19) but made it clear that He, the Christ, would be the Rock upon which the church would rest.[9] The church rests upon that One Foundation, Christ. Every true Christian is a stone in that building, the mystical church. Here the test as to whether or not a person belongs to the church is this—is he resting solely upon the Lord Christ for his salvation?

This concept of the church is quite different from the popular concept of the church as a piece of real estate in which a number of people gather several times a week, presided over by a priest or a pastor. The popular concept of the church is conditioned by culture, history, tradition and background. The true concept is conditioned by what the New Testament says.

The Mirror of the Church

So far we have looked at the church in its *universal aspect*. No man has ever seen the church, thus envisioned, in its entirety for many of its

---

[9] Christ called Himself the *Petra*, a Rock, a mighty outcropping of bedrock granite. The Lord called Peter a *petros*, a piece of rock, a pebble, a stone. That Peter clearly understood the difference is evident from Peter's own statement in his first epistle (1 Peter 2:4-8).

members are already in heaven and many of them are scattered far and wide around the globe. There is, however, a *localized aspect* of the church frequently mentioned in the New Testament. Paul's letter to the Ephesians deals chiefly with the universal aspect of the church, the epistle to the Corinthians deals primarily with the localized aspect of the church. The local church is intended to mirror or reflect the universal church. The New Testament does not see the church broken up into denominations. In fact sectarianism is roundly condemned by Paul (1 Corinthians 1:11-17). But the New Testament does speak of local churches in various cities (Romans 16:5, 15, 16; Revelation 1-2). The epistles of the New Testament were frequently addressed to local churches or to groups of local churches. In fact many of the New Testament epistles were written to correct doctrinal errors, moral problems and spiritual deficiencies in various local churches in apostolic times. The ideal local church should reflect the unity and purpose of the true, mystical, universal church.

The Membership of the Church

The true church is made up only of those who have been truly saved by Christ and united to Him by the Holy Spirit. The membership of the local church should reflect this truth. There is no room for unbelievers in the membership of a local congregation of believers. They should indeed be invited to certain of its functions, especially those convened for evangelism and Bible teaching. But the actual fellowship of the local church is to be composed solely of born again Christians. At the beginning the testimony and power of the local church in Jerusalem was so strong that unsaved people did not dare to join it or seek to join it (Acts 5:11-14). The church exercised strict discipline over its members as the context shows. Such discipline ought still to characterize local congregations of God's people (1 Corinthians 5:1-13).

Every true believer needs the company of other Christians. This fellowship is provided by the local church. It was thus from the very beginning. On the birthday of the church, when three thousand people were saved through Peter's preaching, the immediate result was the forming of a local congregation of believers. We read, "Then they that gladly received his word were baptized: and the same day there were added unto them about three thousand souls. And they continued steadfastly in the apostles doctrine and fellowship, and in breaking of bread and in prayers" (Acts 2:41-42).

According to the New Testament, Christ left two ordinances with His church which are especially prominent in this coming together of believers. These ordinances are *Baptism* and *the Lord's Supper.* The two illustrate the truth of the Christian's relationship to the Lord's death. In the Lord's Supper (the communion service, or eucharist), the Christian depicts Christ's death for him; in baptism he testifies to his death with Christ. Both ordinances play an important part in strengthening the Christian. In the early church, baptism took the form of a public confession of faith in Christ (Matthew 28:19-20; Acts 8:12, 16, 36; 9:18; 10:47; 16:15, 33; 18:8; 19:3). The Lord's Supper sets forth, in the emblems of bread and wine, the death of the Lord Jesus and serves to remind us, whenever the communion table is set, of all that we owe to Him (1 Corinthians 11:23-34).

The Ministry of the Church

The Lord has gifted every Christian with some spiritual abilities which are to be used, in cooperation with other Christians, for the "perfecting of the saints, for the work of the ministry, for the edifying of the body of Christ" (Ephesians 4:11). Numerous gifts are enumerated in the New Testament including, happily enough, that of "helps" (1 Corinthians 12:28). The more prominent ones are listed as "apostles, prophets, evangelists, pastors and teachers" (Ephesians 4:11). *Apostles* and *prophets* were men, especially gifted by the Holy Spirit, to take care of the foundational needs of the church in its early days (Ephesians 2:20; 3:4-5). As such they no longer exist in the church although, in a lesser sense, missionaries and preachers carry on some of their functions. *Evangelists* are men gifted by the Holy Spirit to deal with unbelievers and bring them to a saving knowledge of the Lord Jesus Christ. Of course, every believer is to be a living testimony to the lost and can have the privilege of introducing others to the Savior. Evangelists, however, have a special gift for this type of work. *Pastors* are those gifted to care for the spiritual needs of Christians. They act as spiritual shepherds. *Teachers* are those gifted by the Holy Spirit to make clear to others the truths and doctrines of the Bible.

Local congregations also need the ministry of deacons and elders. *Deacons* are those gifted and spiritually qualified to take care of the more secular and routine matters connected with the congregation (Acts 6:1-7; 1 Timothy 3:8-13). *Elders* (sometimes called "bishops" or "presbyters") are those gifted to take care of the spiritual needs of the congregation as their qualifications so clearly indicate (1 Timothy 3:1-7). Peter classed himself as an elder (1 Peter 5:1-4) and has an interesting comment on the fact that those in this position are not "lords over God's heritage" but examples to the flock.

The Message of the Church

The church is here on earth to represent Christ to a lost world. Its message is to both the saved and to the lost. To those who are saved it unfolds those great truths of the New Testament which are designed to build up Christians in their most holy faith (Jude 20). It teaches "the apostles' doctrine." It expounds the great truths of the Bible in all their length and breadth and height and depth. To those who are lost it proclaims the holiness of God, the way of salvation, the certainty of coming judgment.

The message of the church is based squarely on the Bible. The church has no warrant to add to that message or to subtract from that message. (See, for example, Revelation 22:17-19.) It marks and avoids those who introduce false teaching (Romans 16:17-18; Galatians 1:6-9; Colossians 2:4-23). The message of the church is a Christ-centered message (1 Corinthians 1:23-24) delivered in the power of the Holy Spirit (1 Corinthians 2:4, 13). It includes many cardinal truths such as those concerning Christ. He is the Son of God; He was born of a virgin; He lived a miraculous life; He died an atoning death; He was raised bodily and ascended into heaven, has a high priestly work at the right hand of God and is coming again.

The Mission of the Church

The church is here to evangelize the lost. Its task is not to save the world, for that is not envisioned by the Lord at all for this age. The very word "church" is from the Greek word *ecclesia*, meaning "a company of called-out ones." The thought behind the word is clearly expressed by James at the first church council when, referring to Simon Peter's testimony, he said, "Simeon hath declared how God at the first did visit the Gentiles, to take out of them a people for his name" (Acts 15:14).

A dynamic local church will be a church with a strong evangelistic outreach at home and abroad. There are untold millions still untold in the world today, lost and on their way to a Christless eternity, needing the message of the gospel. The church's mission is to reach these people with the good news that Jesus saves. The Lord gave this great commission to the disciples just prior to His departure for heaven. He said, "All authority is given unto me in heaven and in earth. Go therefore, and teach all nations, baptizing them in the name of the Father, and of the Son, and of the Holy Ghost: teaching them to observe all things whatsoever I have commanded you: and lo, I am with you always, even unto the end of the world" (Matthew 28:18-20).

Every Christian needs to get involved in this mission of the church. We can all go, even if it is to the neighbor across the street or to the person we meet on the bus. We can all pray for the lost, for relatives and friends, for those in far-off lands, for those who are actively engaged in the work of the gospel. We can all give our means to support the missionary activities of the church and thus have a vital share in its outreach. There are scores of passages in the Bible which urge us on to this task. Study the book of Acts. Read Paul's summary of some of his own missionary activities (Romans 15:14-33). Put your hand upon the restless pulse of Paul's passion for souls. In Philippians 3:13 he says, "Brethren . . . this one thing I do, forgetting those things which are behind, and reaching forth unto those things which are before, I press toward the mark for the prize of the high calling in Christ Jesus." When he wrote that, he had already evangelized Galatia, all of western Asia Minor, Macedonia and Greece, having planted churches in scores of cities, won thousands of people to Christ and inspired numerous men and women to become actively engaged in spreading the gospel. He viewed his task as scarcely begun!

Every disciple of the Lord Jesus except one became a missionary and the only one who didn't became a traitor. Every book in the New Testament addressed to a church was addressed to a church in a foreign country planted by the outreach of a growing, dynamic, active, missionary-minded people. Every book in the New Testament addressed to an individual was addressed to a convert of a foreign missionary. The Lord's last words on earth were "You shall receive power, after that the Holy Ghost is come upon you: and you shall be witnesses unto me both in Jerusalem, and in all Judea, and in Samaria, and unto the uttermost part of the earth" (Acts 1:8). These words became the very blueprint of the church as we see it in the book of Acts. The last word of the Holy Spirit in the New Testament shows us God still sounding out the great evangel: Come! (Revelation 22:17).

The Methods of the Church

God's work must be done in God's way. It must be done in God's time and by God's power. Worldly expedients for getting things done have no place in the church. The church is not here to imitate the world, employ its agents, use its methods, ape its programs. The church is here to give the Holy Spirit a vehicle through which He can express the plan and the power of God in this age. The church's methods must be spiritual and not carnal. Paul says, "For the weapons of our warfare are not carnal, but mighty through God to the pulling down of strongholds" (2 Corinthians 10:4).

The church does not lean on the arms of princes. It does not canvass unbelievers for support (1 Corinthians 1:26-29; 2:6-8; 3 John 7). It does not resort to worldly wisdom. The church is planted on earth as on foreign soil. Its roots are in heaven and it draws its support from above. Whenever the church stoops to lower ideals than these, it earns for itself the scorn and disgust of the world and loses power both with God and with men. All history bears testimony to that.

This, then, is the church! In selecting a local church with which to fellowship, look for one which has the marks of a New Testament church. You will not find a perfect church because any local congregation is made up of imperfect people. But you should be able to find one which has most of the marks we have been considering in this lesson.

NOTES

NOTES

NOTES

NOTES